How to Make
PVC PIPE
FURNITURE
for Indoors and Outdoors

How to Make

PVC PIPE FURNITURE

for Indoors and Outdoors

From The Family Workshop
By Ed and Stevie Baldwin

DOUBLEDAY

NEW YORK LONDON TORONTO SYDNEY AUCKLAND

PREFACE

As a do-it-yourselfer, you're probably as skeptical as we are when you read about how "easy" it is to build this or that project. Take it from one pair who has been down every do-it-yourself path, you will find none of these problems in working with PVC pipe! This stuff is truly easy to use, and requires no tools more complex than a hack saw and, occasionally, an electric drill. We've simplified the instructions and assembly diagrams so you can breeze right through any project that catches your fancy. We know you'll find that working with PVC is a piece of cake. And that's the truth!

We'd like to offer special thanks to Genova, Inc., of Davison, Michigan, manufacturers of plastic plumbing materials. They shipped us an unending supply of high-quality pipe, fittings, solvent cement, special paint, and unerring advice. Thanks also to the folks at Fabricut, Inc., of Tulsa, Oklahoma, who provided the handsome upholstery fabric for the sofa and easy chair. We used a Singer Stylist 834 sewing machine for all the fabric assemblies.

Dedicated in loving memory to Norman Hoss, a very special individual.

Created by The Family Workshop, Inc.
Editorial Director: Jan Weberling
Editors: Suzi West, Mike McUsic
Art Director: Dale Crain
Production Artists: Roberta Taff, Janice Harris Burstall, Wanda Young
Typography: Deborah Gahm
Creative Director: April Bail
Project Designs: Ed and Stevie Baldwin, D. J. Olin, Roberta Taff, and April Bail
Photography: Bill Welch

The information in this book is true and complete to the best of our knowledge. All recommendations are made without guarantees on the part of the authors or Doubleday & Company, Inc., who disclaim all liability in connection with the use of this information.

Additional craft patterns are available from The Family Workshop, Inc. For a catalog, send $2.95 to: The Family Workshop, Department 10022, P. O. Box 1000, Bixby, Oklahoma 74008

PUBLISHED BY DOUBLEDAY
a division of Bantam Doubleday Dell Publishing Group, Inc.
666 Fifth Avenue, New York, New York 10103

DOUBLEDAY and the portrayal of an anchor with a dolphin are trademarks
of Doubleday, a division of Bantam Doubleday Dell Publishing Group, Inc.

Library of Congress Cataloging in Publication Data
Baldwin, Ed.
    How to make PVC pipe furniture, for indoors and outdoors.
    1. Plastic furniture. 2. Plastics craft. 3. Polyvinyl chloride.   I. Baldwin, Stevie.
II. Title. III. Title: PVC pipe furniture, for indoors and outdoors.
TT297.5.B33   1985   684.1'06   85-6871
ISBN 0-385-23219-5

Contents

Read the "Tips & Techniques" section before beginning work on any project!

Tips & Techniques

If you liked erector sets as a child, you'll love working with plastic pipe. But even if erector sets were not your idea of a good time, you're bound to be impressed at how easy it is to construct attractive, sturdy, indoor/outdoor furniture from this material.

General characteristics

Plastic pipe is used for most plumbing jobs these days because it is virtually impervious to the elements. It is extremely strong, will not rust or decay, and is easy to cut and join using only a hand saw and special cement. These same properties make it an excellent material for furniture building.

There are several different types of plastic pipe, made according to various chemical formulas. The two strongest are PVC (polyvinyl chloride) and CPVC (chlorinated polyvinyl chloride). CPVC is the more expensive of the two.

In a way, these materials are very much like human bone. They can take a lot of straight-on pressure, but will break or crack when bent too far. Extremely high temperatures will cause the pipe to soften. CPVC will remain hard at higher temperatures than PVC, but even PVC will withstand a hotter temperature (approximately 120 degrees Fahrenheit) than that to which your furniture will normally be exposed. Extremely low temperatures will not harm plastic pipe, but will make it brittle. Under freezing conditions, a sharp knock against something hard can cause the pipe to crack or shatter.

Pipe and fittings

You will be working with straight pipe and with contoured fittings of various shapes. The fittings are used to join the straight lengths of pipe.

Figure A shows the fittings that we used for the projects in this book. All PVC fittings are female, fitting around rather than inside the straight pipe. As you will see when you make your first purchase, some fittings are manufactured with a "collar" at each opening and some are not. The fittings shown in **Figure A** do have collars, but it's not necessary to purchase this kind. The collars have no bearing on fit, and will make no difference in the assembly of the projects. In fact, the assembly diagrams in this book show fittings without collars, so you'll be able to read them more easily.

There are many more types of fittings than the ones shown here. You will find, for instance, three different types of 90-degree angle fittings. One is a standard 90-degree fitting, and is the type we used throughout the book. It is shown in **Figure A**. Another type is called a "90-degree short turn," and is shorter than the standard. A third type is called a "90-degree long sweep," and is longer than the standard. Obviously, if you use either the shorter or longer fitting in place of the standard, it will affect the size of the finished project.

There are also at least two types of double-T fittings. We used the double-T shown in **Figure A**, not a "cross" fitting, which is the same shape but with shorter ends. Be aware, also, that there is a difference between a standard T-fitting and what is called a "double 90." They look quite similar, but we used the standard T-fitting shown in **Figure A**.

Straight pipe is sized by internal diameter. A "1-inch" pipe has in inner diameter of 1 inch, give or take a little. (That's called the "tolerance.") Fitting sizes are determined by the sizes of pipe that they join, not by any measurement of the fitting itself. Thus, a fitting that accommodates 1-inch pipes is called a 1-inch fitting, even though the inner diameter of the fitting does not measure 1 inch.

Because of that little bugaboo called tolerance, and because manufacturers may vary somewhat on standard sizes, it's a good idea to test all pipe and fittings before you fork over the cash and leave the store. The pipe should slide easily into the fitting, but you should not be able to rock it up and down within the fitting. If it is too loose or too tight, simply ask for another fitting.

Standard PVC pipe is graded according to its strength and normal use in various plumbing jobs. We used "schedule 40" pipe and fittings for most of the projects in this book. It is quite strong, and has held up well under unusually lengthy "tests" conducted by certain staff members, especially on items like the hammock and sling chair!

You may find that some home centers carry a product called "furniture-grade" PVC. The pipe and fittings are manufactured in decorator colors, and generally cost more than standard PVC plumbing pipe. Its biggest advantage, claim the makers, is that it contains a substance that blocks the ultraviolet rays of the sun. Their contention is that normal plumbing pipe deteriorates over time, when it is left outdoors, and eventually becomes very brittle – prone to snap when hefty Uncle Bob takes a seat in your handsome PVC lawn chair. We're not scientists, so we can't verify or disprove their theory in the lab. But we can report on our experience. A few of the projects in this book were assembled as long ago as 1981, have been on our patio ever since, and still are holding up just fine. You may wish to seek out furniture-grade pipe for the projects you build, or simply paint the projects you make from standard PVC plumbing pipe, to protect them from the sun's rays.

Securing the joints

When PVC pipe is used for plumbing, the joints are sealed with a special solvent cement that sets off a chemical reaction, permanently welding the pipe and fittings together. This keeps pressurized water from leaking all over your house. Unless you plan to run water through your furniture (a fountain chair, perhaps?), you have the option of securing the joints with self-tapping sheet metal screws. It takes more time to use screws than solvent cement, but it does allow you to disassemble the structure, if and when you want to.

If you opt for cemented joints, be sure to purchase the particular solvent cement made for use with the type of pipe you buy. Even within this limitation, you will have a choice of cements, each with a different set-up time. The one with the longest set-up time is the easiest to use because it allows an extra minute or two for adjustments before the joint is locked for all eternity.

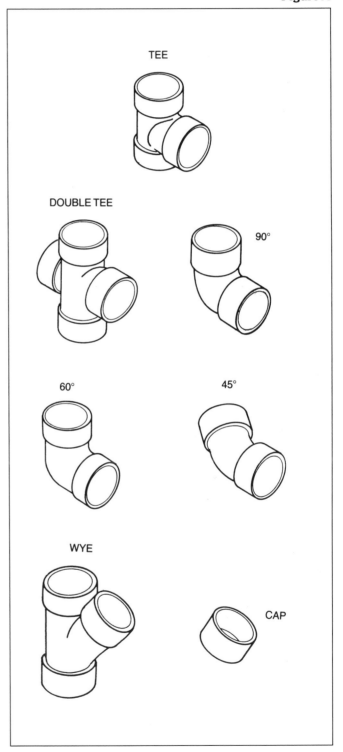

Figure A

TEE

DOUBLE TEE

90°

60°

45°

WYE

CAP

And we do mean all eternity. There is no way to disassemble a cemented joint, short of sawing off the pipe and starting over again with new pieces. You should dry assemble each project to make sure that all parts fit together properly before cementing them. You may have to trim some of the pieces slightly to get a proper fit, but be sure that all pieces are inserted into the fittings as far as they will go before you decide they need trimming. Keep in mind that a cemented project that is too large to fit through the door will be a permanent resident of the room in which it is built.

If you use cement, read the manufacturer's instructions carefully. Most brands require you to prepare the portion of pipe that will be inserted into the fitting, and the inside of the fitting where it will meet the pipe. The preparation consists of sanding lightly and then applying PVC cleaner, to remove the protective coating and any grime or finger oil. When the pipe and fittings are clean, simply apply the cement, insert the pipe into the fitting, and give it a twist or two to force out air bubbles. Work in a well ventilated area, as the fumes are noxious, to say the least!

If you want to be able to disassemble the project, do not use cement. Instead, secure each joint with two self-tapping sheet metal screws. To insert each screw, drill a hole through the assembled joint using a drill bit that is slightly smaller in diameter than the screw shank. Disassemble the joint and enlarge the hole in the fitting only, using a bit that is larger than the screw shank but smaller than the screw head. Then simply reassemble the joint and insert the screw. It's a good idea to mark each corresponding pipe and fitting with a code letter, to facilitate reassembly when you port your portable piece of furniture.

Figure B

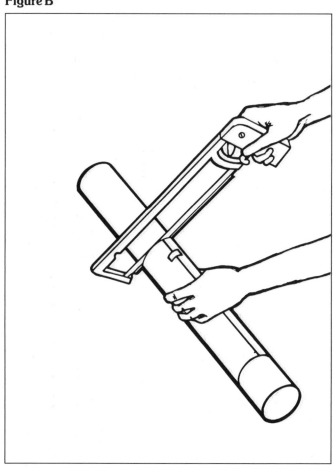

Cutting and drilling

PVC pipe is sold in standard lengths. You'll have to cut the pipe into the shorter pieces specified for each project. There are no special tricks to cutting the pipe. Just mark off the lengths and cut in as straight a line as possible, so the pipe will fit squarely into the fitting. If you wrap a straight piece of paper around the pipe at the point you wish to cut, and tape the paper in place, you can follow the edge with your saw to get a nice square cut (**Figure B**).

Figure C

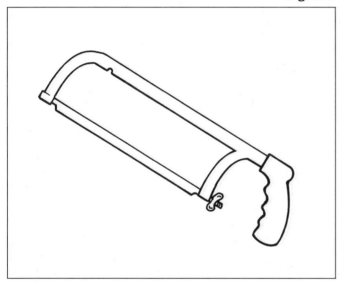

Figure D

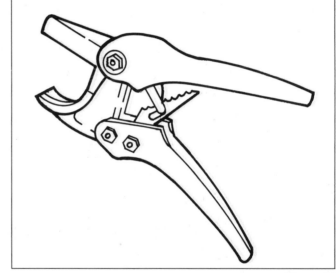

Figure E

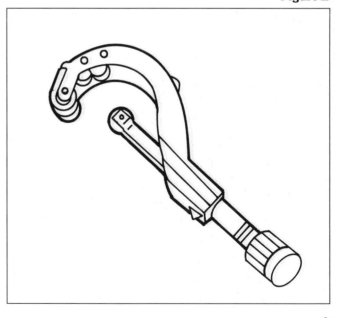

We suggest that you mark off all of the required lengths, starting with the longest ones, before you begin to cut. There will be much less waste this way. File off any burrs or rough spots on the cut ends.

You can use any type of saw with a fine-toothed blade to cut plastic pipe. A hack saw with a fine-toothed metal blade (**Figure C**) will work just fine. If you have access to a band saw, it will speed the cutting process. There is a gadget called a "ratchet shears" (**Figure D**) that is made *especially* for cutting plastic pipe. It works much like scissors. We tested it, and it seems to work well, but we prefer the band saw. We also tested a wheel-blade cutter (**Figure E**), but found it to be more trouble than it was worth.

In this book, the instructions for each project include a list of the required lengths of straight pipe. The various lengths and fittings are identified by code letters on the list. The code letters, in turn, appear on the assembly diagrams. If you label each length as you cut, and label each fitting, you'll know at a glance which goes where when you're deep in the throes of the assembly process.

Figure F

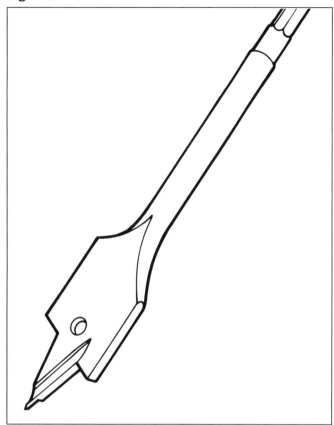

Figure G

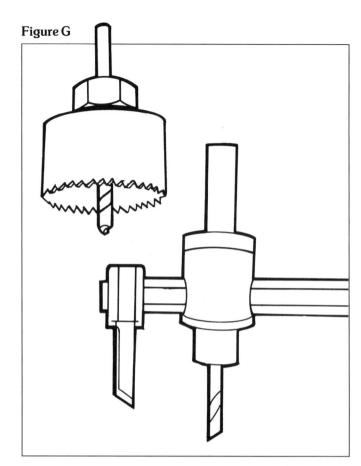

There are projects in this book that require you to drill holes in the pipe and fittings. Again, there are no special tricks. You can use a hand-held power drill with a normal metal or wood bit. For large holes, use a spade bit with your hand-held drill (**Figure F**), or use a hole saw or fly cutter attachment on a drill press (**Figure G**).

Please take special note of the following tip. We have specified the diameter of each hole to be drilled, but you will find that the specified diameters are not generally correct. Here's why: As we said before, pipe is sized by internal diameter. While the internal diameter of all 1-inch pipe will always measure very close to 1 inch, the external diameter will vary greatly from brand to brand and from grade to grade. Some pipe simply has thicker walls. So, you can see that while one type of 1-inch pipe might have an external diameter of 1¼ inches, another type might have an external diameter of 1½ inches. In order to eliminate a lot of excess verbiage when specifying the diameters of the holes you need to drill, we have always called for a hole the same size as or just slightly larger than the INTERNAL diameter of the pipe that will be inserted into the hole. You can drill the holes to the sizes specified and then enlarge them using a drill or file, or you can measure the EXTERNAL diameter of the pipe that will be inserted into the hole and drill the hole to that size.

Finishing

PVC pipe and fittings are manufactured for general use in four colors: beige, white, gray, and black. If you prefer a different color, just add paint. Almost any type of paint will work, but oil-based paint is best. There are paints made especially for use with plastic pipe. Whatever type of paint you use, spraying gives a smoother look than brushing.

PVC is harder than any paint, so chips or scratches will allow the base color to show through. It is important to prepare the surface before painting. First, clean the pipe with turpentine or PVC cleaner to remove dirt and oily residues. Add a coat of primer, allow it to dry, and then paint. Two thin coats of paint will stand up better than one thick one. We suggest that you assemble the project before you do any surface preparation or painting.

To repair a spot where the paint has been chipped or scratched, first sand the spot and the area immediately surrounding it. Add a thin coat of primer, allow it to dry, and sand again using ultra-fine sandpaper. Then repaint. To finish the repair job, sand the area with ultra-fine sandpaper, paying special attention to the outlines, and then shine with jeweler's polish.

If you opt not to paint, you'll have to decide how to treat the printed information (manufacturer's name, size, etc.) that appears on many brands of pipe and fittings. You can sometimes turn the pieces so that the printing is hidden on the assembled project, or you might want to display it prominently

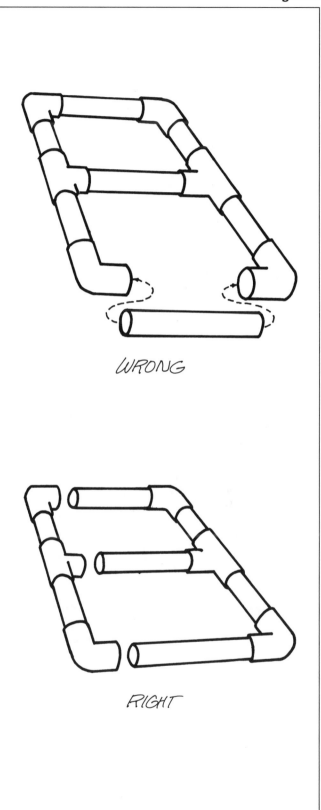

for a funky look. Then again, you may wish to do away with it entirely. The printing can be taken off using acetone, finger-nail polish remover, automotive choke cleaner, or paint remover. Pour the liquid on a clean rag and rub along the printing in one direction only, so you do not smear the ink all over the pipe.

The surface of PVC pipe will roughen over time, but scratches will not show if the pipe is not painted. If you want a high-gloss finish, use ultra-fine sandpaper followed by jeweler's polish. Both painted and unpainted PVC can be finished with wax.

Original designs

When you see how easy it is to build handsome furnishings from PVC pipe, you may be inspired to create some original designs. If so, keep a few simple rules in mind. First, it's important to make a diagram so you'll know if the design will work. From the diagram, you can also compute how much pipe and how many of the various fittings you'll need. Don't forget to include fitting allowances (the amount on each end of each pipe that is hidden inside the fitting) when figuring the amount of straight pipe you'll need.

Work out the step-by-step assembly on paper also, to avoid getting yourself into an impossible situation with the last piece of pipe. **Figure H** shows an example of what we mean. The assembly procedure in the first drawing is impossible because you cannot bend the pipe in order to get it between the two fittings.

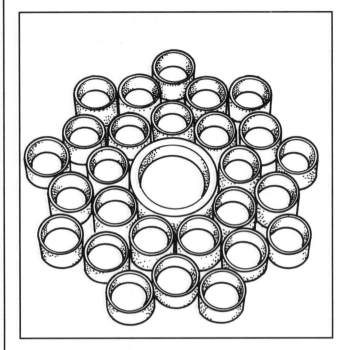

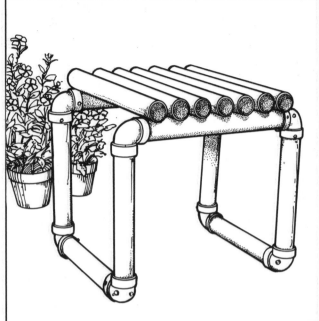

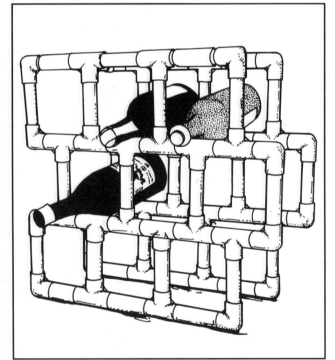

Practice Projects

The projects in this section were designed to give you practice in cutting, joining, and drilling plastic pipe. All are relatively simple, but useful, items. Read the "Tips & Techniques" section of this book before you begin work on any project.

Figure A

Trivet

Use this handy little item to protect your tabletop from hot dishes. Made from beige pipe, it resembles the Oriental versions made from bamboo. Once you get the idea, you can design your own trivets in different shapes.

Materials

⅜-inch length of straight 1¼-inch PVC pipe.
14-inch length of straight ¾-inch CPVC pipe.
PVC solvent cement.

Cutting and assembly

The trivet consists of twenty-eight slices of pipe that are glued together (**Figure C**).

1. Cut the ¾-inch pipe into twenty-seven slices, each ⅜ inch thick.

2. Place the slice of 1¼-inch pipe on a flat surface, and arrange nine of the smaller slices around it (**Figure A**). Glue the smaller slices to the larger one and to each other.

3. Make a second ring of smaller slices around the first ring (**Figure B**). Glue them to the slices in the first ring.

4. Make a third ring of slices around the second ring (**Figure C**), and glue them in place.

Figure B

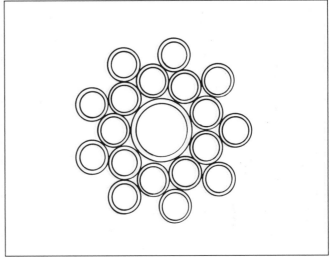

Figure C

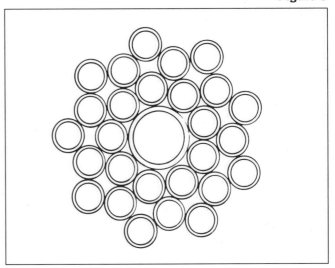

Garden Seat

This little one-person bench is a real snap to make. Overall dimensions are 19 x 16 x 19 inches. Put a pillow on top to use it as a seat or footstool, or temporarily replace the pillow with a tray to use it as an end table!

Figure A

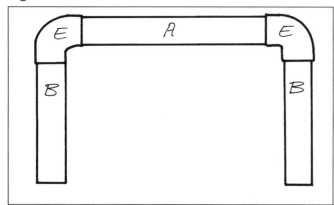

Figure B

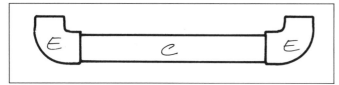

Figure C

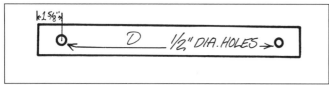

Materials

20 feet of straight 1½-inch PVC pipe.
1½-inch PVC fittings: eight 90-degree angle joints.
PVC solvent cement or thirty-two No. 6 gauge self-tapping sheet metal screws, each ¾ inch long.
Fourteen No. 6 gauge sheet metal screws, each ½ inch long.

Assembling the frame

The garden seat consists of two identical end sections (**Figure A**), two span sections (**Figure B**), and seven seat bars. The assembled garden seat is shown in **Figure D**.

Figure D

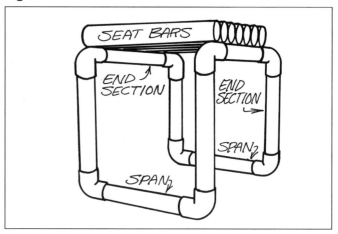

1. The lengths of straight pipe listed below were calculated on the basis of ¾-inch fitting allowances. Check the depth of each fitting and recalculate the lengths, if necessary, to compensate for the difference on each end. (Note: Do not alter the length of the **D** pieces.) Cut and label the lengths of straight pipe. Label the fittings as listed.

Part	Length	Quantity
A	16½ inches	2
B	12¾ inches	4
C	12¼ inches	2
D	17 inches	7
Fittings:		
E	90-degree joint	

2. Assemble two end sections as shown in **Figure A**.
3. Assemble two span sections as shown in **Figure B**.
4. Join the two end sections using the two span sections. Refer to **Figure D** if you're not sure how this goes.

Adding the seat bars

1. Each seat bar (**D**) must be drilled to accommodate the screws that will hold it in place on the frame. Draw a straight line along one **D** piece, from end to end, using a felt-tip marker. Drill two ½-inch-diameter holes into the pipe, placing the center of each hole on the line and 1⅝ inches from the end, as shown in **Figure C**.
2. Change your drill bit to a size that is slightly smaller than the diameter of the ½-inch screw shanks. Drill a hole through the pipe directly opposite each larger hole. Drill each remaining **D** piece in the same manner.
3. The assembled frame with the seat bars attached is shown in **Figure D**. Place the seven **D** pieces across the top of the frame as shown. They should all be placed over the top frame pipes between the fittings. Space them evenly, leaving a short gap between each seat bar, and rotate them so that the larger holes are on top. To secure each bar, insert a screw through the bottom of the bar, into the pipe below it, at each end. You can insert your screwdriver down through the larger holes in the tops of the bars.

Wine Rack

This handy rack will hold nine bottles of your favorite elixir. It's made primarily of T-joints, so you'll get lots of practice in joining and cutting short lengths of straight pipe.

Materials

18 feet of straight ¾-inch CPVC pipe.
¾-inch CPVC fittings: forty T-joints and sixteen 90-degree angle joints.
CPVC solvent cement.

Cutting the pipe

The lengths of straight pipe listed below were calculated on the basis of ⅝-inch fitting allowances. Check the depth of the fittings you purchased and recalculate the lengths, if necessary, to compensate for the difference on each end. Cut and label the lengths of pipe. Label the fittings as listed.

Part	Length	Quantity
A	4 inches	28
B	1⁷⁄₁₆ inches	44
C	5½ inches	4

Fittings:	
D	T-joint
E	90-degree joint

Assembly

The wine rack consists of two identical frame sections that are joined by four crossbars in the final assembly. Each of the frame sections consists of four vertical assemblies (**Figures A** through **D**) and twelve crossbars. One assembled frame section is shown in **Figure E**, and the completed rack is shown in **Figure F**.

1. Begin by building the first vertical assembly for one of the frame sections, following the diagram in **Figure A**. Simply put the pieces and fittings together in the order shown. The short **B** pieces will show only slightly between the fittings they join. Be sure to insert the pipes into the fittings as far as they will go, or the vertical assemblies will not match up. If you tap each piece lightly with a hammer as you assemble them, you'll be sure of a tight fit. In addition, be sure that each fitting faces the direction shown on the diagram.

2. Build the second vertical assembly as shown in **Figure B**. Again, be sure that each fitting faces the direction shown.

Figure A

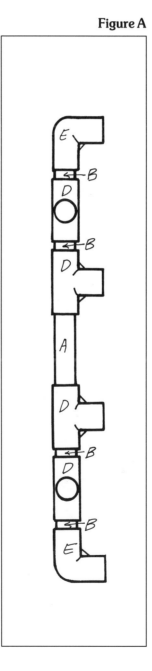

Figure B

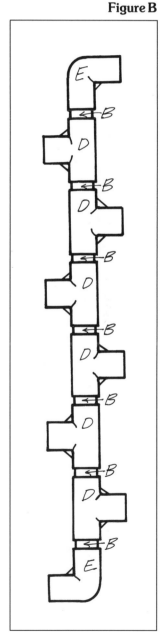

Figure E

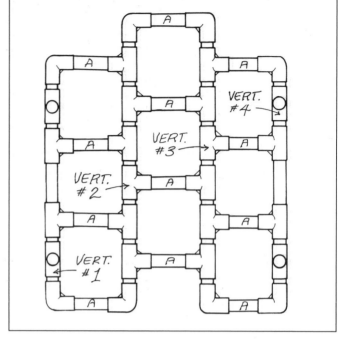

Figure C

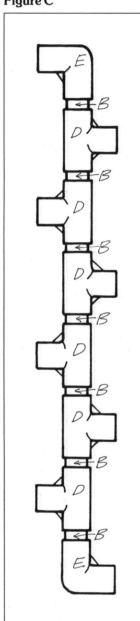

Figure D

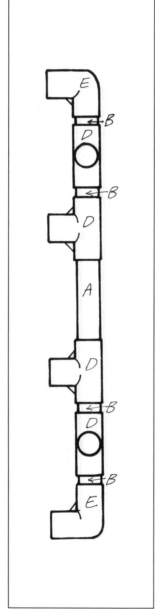

Figure F

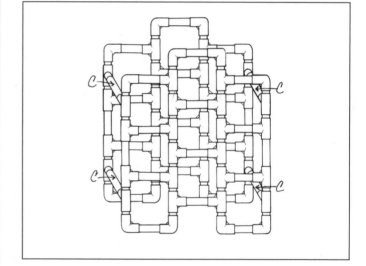

4. Build the fourth vertical assembly as shown in **Figure D**. It is a mirror image of the one you built in step 1.

5. One assembled frame section is shown in **Figure E**. Join the four vertical assemblies, as shown, using twelve **A** pieces. To do this properly, first insert an **A** piece into each of the right-facing **D** fittings on the first vertical assembly. Install the second vertical assembly on the ends of these **A** pieces. Insert an **A** piece into each of the remaining open **D** fittings on the second assembly, and install the third vertical, etc.

6. Repeat the procedures in steps 1 through 5 to assemble a second identical frame section.

7. The assembled rack is shown in **Figure F**. Insert a **C** piece into each of the remaining open **D** fittings in one frame section. Install the other frame section as shown.

3. Build the third vertical assembly as shown in **Figure C**. This assembly is a mirror image of the one you built in step 2. It's exactly the same, but each fitting is turned in the opposite direction.

Headboard or Trellis

This headboard was designed to fit a standard twin bed. You don't need a frame to go with it — simply place it between the head of the bed and the wall, or connect it to the existing metal frame using clamps. Or, plant the structure in your yard and use it as a trellis.

Materials

12 feet of straight 1½-inch PVC pipe.

1½-inch PVC fittings: three 45-degree angle joints, two T-joints, and two end caps. The end caps are unnecessary if you use the structure as a trellis.

14 feet of straight ¾-inch CPVC pipe.

PVC solvent cement, or twenty-eight No. 6 gauge self-tapping sheet metal screws, each ¾ inch long.

Cutting the pipe

1. The lengths of straight 1½-inch pipe listed below were calculated on the basis of ¾-inch fitting allowances. Check the depth of each fitting and recalculate the lengths, if necessary, to compensate for the difference on each end. Cut and label the lengths of pipe. Label the fittings as listed.

Part	Length	Quantity
A	38½ inches	1
B	7½ inches	2
C	22⅛ inches	2
D	19 inches	2

Fittings:

Part	Length	
E	45-degree joint	
F	T-joint	
G	End cap	

2. Cut the lengths of straight ¾-inch pipe listed below. There's no need to recalculate for fitting allowances.

Part	Length	Quantity
H	22 inches	1
J	19½ inches	2
K	17½ inches	2
L	16 inches	2
M	17 inches	2

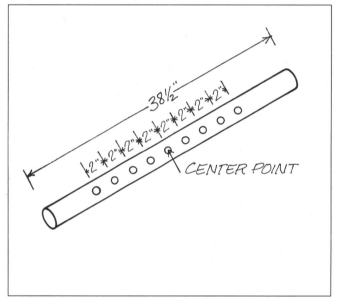

Figure A

3. The **A** piece must be drilled to accommodate the ¾-inch pipes that will serve as the "rays" of the headboard. The drilling points are illustrated in **Figure A**. Draw a straight line along the pipe, from end to end. Mark the center point on the line. Measure 2 inches from the center point, on each side, and mark these points. Continue to measure and mark at 2-inch intervals until there are nine drilling points marked on the pipe: one at the center and four on each side of the center point. Drill a hole into the pipe at each point, using a bit that matches the outer diameter of the ¾-inch pipe you purchased. (Remember, the ¾-inch pipe measures ¾ inch on the *inside*. It will measure ⅞ to 1 inch along the outside diameter.) Drill only through one "side" of the pipe — do not continue to drill out the other side.

Figure B

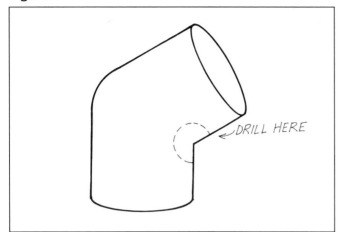

Figure C

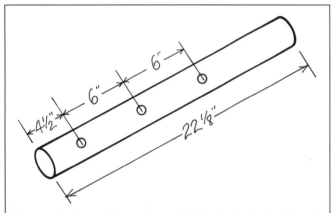

Figure D

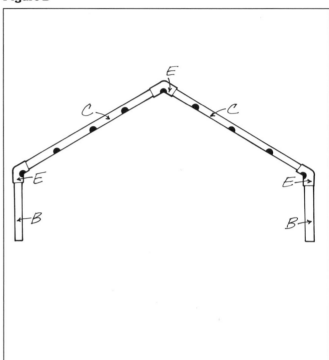

Figure E

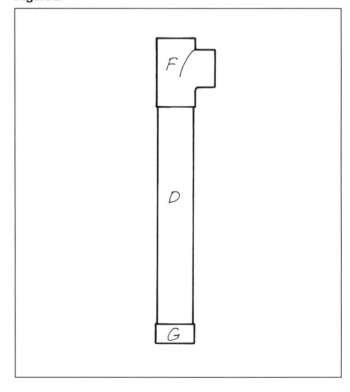

4. Each of the **E** fittings must also be drilled. Use the same size bit to drill a hole into one of the fittings at the exact center of the inside corner, as shown in **Figure B**. Do not drill all the way through and out the other side. Drill each of the **E** fittings in this manner.

5. Finally, each of the **C** pieces must be drilled as shown in **Figure C**. Draw a straight line along each **C** piece, from end to end. Measure 4½ inches from one end of the pipe and place a mark on the line at this point. (Note: The 4½-inch distance is based on a ¾-inch fitting allowance. If the fitting allowance on the 45-degree joints is different, recalculate this distance to compensate. For the remaining points on this line, it is not necessary to recalculate.) Measure 6 inches from the first point and make a second mark. Measure 6 inches from the second point and make a third mark. Drill a hole into the pipe at each point, using the same size bit. Again, drill through one side of the pipe only. Drill the remaining **C** piece in the same manner. The end of each **C** piece closest to the first point will be the upper end of the pipe. Remember this when you are assembling the headboard.

Assembly

1. Assemble the peak of the headboard (**Figure D**).
2. Assemble one vertical leg as shown in **Figure E**.
3. Assemble a second vertical leg in the same manner.

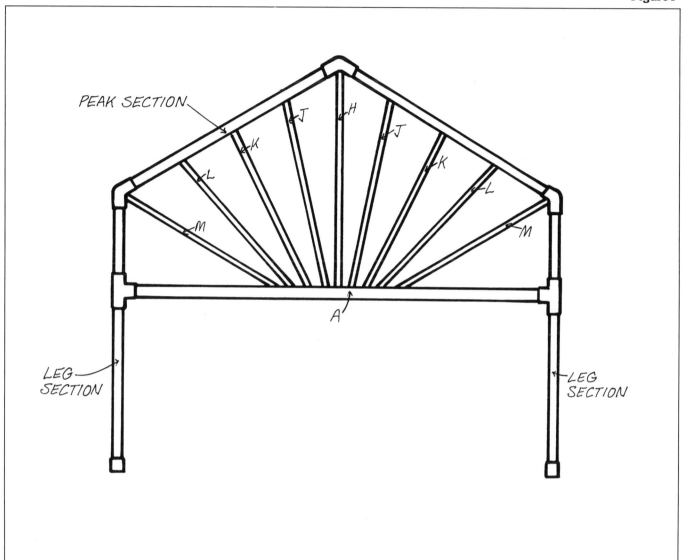

PEAK SECTION

LEG SECTION

LEG SECTION

4. The assembled headboard is shown in **Figure F**. As you can see, the ¾-inch pipes that form the rays are set in at various angles, so you'll have to enlarge the holes slightly, some on one side, some on the other, to get a good fit. Begin by temporarily assembling the outer frame structure. To do this, simply join the two leg assemblies using the long **A** piece, and then add the peak structure. Place the entire frame on a flat surface. Be sure that the pieces are turned so that the holes for the ray pipes are facing the proper directions. Place each of the ¾-inch ray pipes on top, in the positions shown in **Figure F**, aligning the ends with the holes you drilled. The holes for the center ray will not have to be altered. Mark the side

of each hole that will have to be enlarged, and use a drill or a penknife to alter the holes. The hole closest to each end of the **A** piece will give you the most trouble, because the angle is so great. The easiest way to enlarge this hole is to use a ⅞-inch bit, and clamp the drill in a vise (or use a drill press). Ease the pipe down onto the drill bit, inserting it into the existing hole, and then slowly angle the pipe. Watch closely, so you don't overdo it. The hole will have to be quite long to accommodate the angle of the pipe.

5. Remove the peak assembly, insert the ray pipes into the holes along the **A** piece, and then reinstall the peak assembly, guiding the rays into the holes. You may have to work with it a bit to get a good fit.

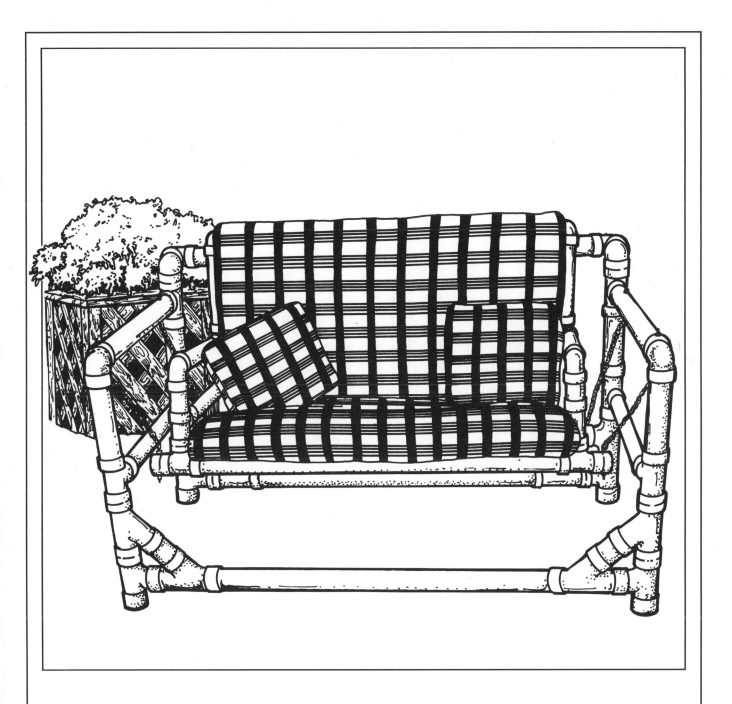

Glider

What a wonderful way to catch the evening breezes! This glider is easy to build and easy to move around the yard, so you can take advantage of shade and prevailing winds. If you've priced one in a store lately, you'll be doubly pleased. Overall dimensions are 33 x 34 x 58 inches. The simple, stuffed-fabric cushion can be stitched up by anyone who can find the "on" switch of a sewing machine.

Figure A

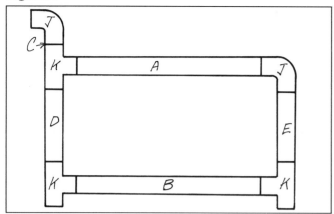

Figure B

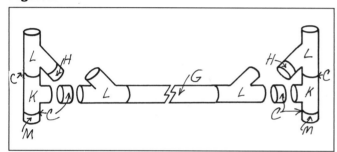

Figure C

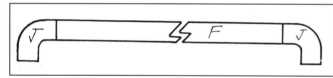

Materials

For the frame:

26 feet of straight 2-inch PVC pipe.

2-inch PVC fittings: six 90-degree angle joints, ten T-joints, eight Y-joints, and four end caps.

PVC solvent cement or several large handfuls of self-tapping sheet metal screws, each 1 inch long.

For the seat:

20 feet of straight 1½-inch PVC pipe.

36 feet of straight ¾-inch CPVC pipe.

1½-inch PVC fittings: four 90-degree angle joints, ten T-joints, and four end caps.

PVC solvent cement or approximately 100 self-tapping sheet metal screws, each ¾ or 1 inch long.

Eight rustproof eyebolts, each 4 inches long with a 1-inch-diameter eye, and each with a washer and nut. You'll need four cap nuts, in addition to the standard nuts.

Four 8-inch lengths of No. 8 or heavier chain. This will be used to hang the seat from the frame, so if you eat a lot you'll want heavier chain.

Eight connecting links, one size larger than the chain. These will be used to connect the lengths of chain to the eyebolts. As an alternative, you can pry open the eye of each bolt,

insert the end link of the chain, and reclose the eye. Large eyebolts are not easy to pry open, however, so you may prefer to use the connecting links. We do not recommend S-hooks because they're likely to fail when the action gets heavy.

For the cushion and pillows:

4 yards of 60-inch-wide fabric. We used a heavy cotton fabric with a large, colorful floral print.

3 yards of 1-inch-wide ribbon in a color that coordinates with the fabric.

Two packages of standard quilt batting.

One pound of polyester fiberfill.

Heavy-duty thread.

Building the frame

The frame is a freestanding structure from which the glider seat hangs. Five separate sections make up the frame: two identical side sections (**Figure A**), two identical leg sections (**Figure B**), and a back section (**Figure C**). The entire assembled frame is shown in **Figure D**.

1. The required lengths of straight 2-inch pipe are listed below. They were calculated on the basis of ¾-inch fitting allowances. Check the depth of each 2-inch fitting and, if necessary, recalculate the lengths to compensate for the difference on each end. Cut and label the pieces of straight pipe. Label the 2-inch fittings as listed.

Part	Length	Quantity
A	21¾ inches	2
B	20¾ inches	2
C	1⅜ inches	20
D	8 inches	2
E	9¼ inches	2
F	52½ inches	1
G	38 inches	2
H	3½ inches	4
Fittings:		
J	90-degree joint	
K	T-joint	
L	Y-joint	
M	End cap	

2. Build one side section as shown in **Figure A**. First, assemble the vertical portion on the left side of the diagram, using a short **C** piece to connect the **J** and **K** fittings at the top. (This will be a back corner post of the frame.) Add the horizontal **A** and **B** pieces. Then assemble the vertical portion on the right side of the diagram and slip it in place.

3. Assemble an identical side section.

4. Assemble one leg section (**Figure B**). Begin with the two end portions, using a short **C** piece between fittings where indicated. Assemble the horizontal center portion and then join it to the end portions, using a short **C** piece where indicated at each end.

5. Assemble an identical leg section.

6. Assemble the back section as shown in **Figure C**.

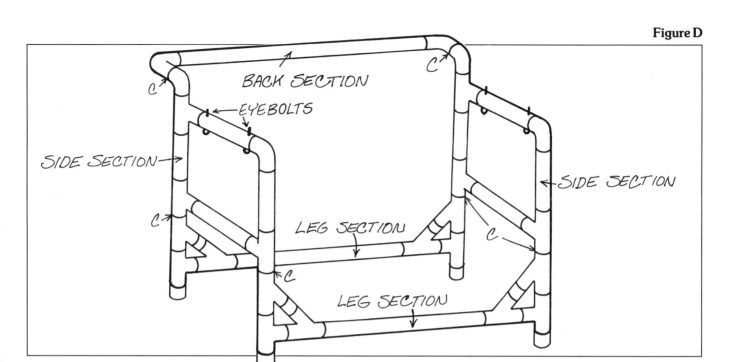

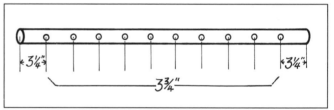

7. The assembled frame is shown in **Figure D**. Begin by attaching the two leg sections to one side section. Use a short **C** piece to connect each **K** fitting at the bottom of the side section to the **L** fitting at the top of the leg section. Attach the opposite end of each leg section to the remaining side section in the same manner. The back section connects the two side sections at the top. Use a short **C** piece to join the two **J** fittings at each end.

8. To accommodate the eyebolts, drill two holes through the **A** piece on each end of the frame (**Figure D**). Use a drill bit just slightly larger than the diameter of the bolt shank and drill straight down through the pipe, in one side and out the other. Place one hole close to the **J** fitting at the front, and the second hole 3 inches from the **K** fitting at the back. Insert the eyebolts from the bottom up and secure each one with a washer, a standard nut, and a cap nut.

Building the seat

The glider seat consists of a back section (**Figure F**) and a front section (**Figure G**), which are joined by crossbars and seat support bars. The assembled seat is shown in **Figure H**.

1. Cut and label the lengths of straight 1½-inch pipe listed below. They were calculated on the basis of ¾-inch fitting allowances. Check the depth of each 1½-inch fitting and recalculate the lengths, if necessary.

Part	Length	Quantity
A	14⅛ inches	2
B	3½ inches	4
C	13¼ inches	2
D	3 inches	2
E	9¾ inches	2
F	1⅜ inches	6
G	40⅛ inches	3

2. Cut the lengths of ¾-inch CPVC pipe listed below. No adjustment is necessary to compensate for fitting allowances. Label the 1½-inch fittings as listed.

Part	Length	Quantity
H	25 inches	10
J	17 inches	11
Fittings:		
K	90-degree joint	
L	T-joint	
M	End cap	

3. The three **G** pieces must be drilled to accommodate the pieces of ¾-inch pipe, which will serve as seat support bars and back support bars. Use a ⅞-inch-diameter drill bit for all of the holes. One of the **G** pieces will be the top horizontal bar of the back section (**Figure F**). Draw a straight line along this piece from end to end. Drill ten holes where indicated in **Figure E**, placing the center of each hole on the line. Drill through one "side" of the pipe only; do not continue drilling completely through the other side of the pipe. (Note: The distance from each end of the pipe to the center of the closest hole depends on the length of the fitting allowance. The 3¼-inch measurement specified on the diagram includes our ¾-inch allowance. Recalculate this measurement if you are working with a different allowance. The 3¾-inch measurement between holes will not change.)

Figure F

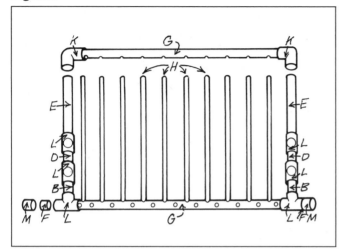

Figure G

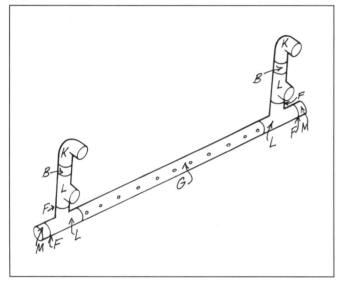

Figure H

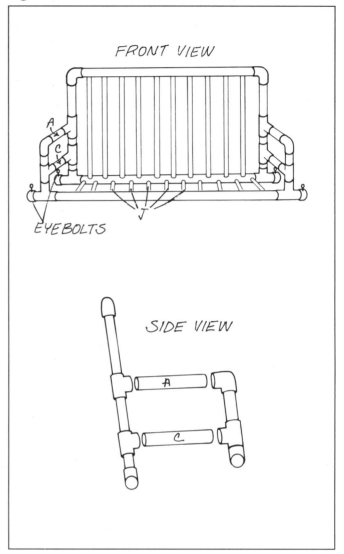

4. A second **G** piece will be the bottom horizontal bar of the back section. You'll need to drill two lines of holes in this piece: one to accommodate the lower ends of the back support bars, and one to accommodate the seat support bars. To drill the holes for the back support bars, draw a straight line along the pipe from end to end. Drill ten holes along this line, spacing them as you did the holes in step 3. To drill the holes for the seat support bars, draw a second straight line from end to end, one-quarter of the way around the pipe from the first line. Drill eleven holes along this line: place the center of the first hole 1¼ inches from one end, place the centers of the next nine holes midway between the holes you drilled along the first line, and place the center of the last hole 1¼ inches from the opposite end. (Note: Recalculate the measurement from each end of the pipe to the closest hole if necessary.)

5. The third **G** piece will be the bottom horizontal bar of the front section (**Figure G**). It is drilled to accommodate the seat support bars. Draw a straight line along this piece from end to end and drill eleven holes, spacing them as you did the second line of holes in step 4.

6. Assemble the back section as shown in **Figure F**. Begin with the lower horizontal portion, using the **G** piece that has two lines of holes. Use a short **F** piece to join the **L** and **M** fittings on each end. Add the vertical portion on each side, and then fit the ten **H** pieces (back support bars) into the holes along the top of the **G** piece. Finally, assemble the upper horizontal portion, using the **G** piece that has ten holes. Add this portion to the lower assembly, inserting the ends of the **H** pieces into the holes. Examine your work to make sure that the open ends of the **L** fittings and the eleven empty holes in the lower **G** piece are all facing the same direction.

7. Assemble the front section as shown in **Figure G**, using a short **F** piece wherever two fittings butt together. Be sure that the line of holes along the **G** piece and the open ends of the **L** and **K** fittings all face the same direction.

24

Figure I

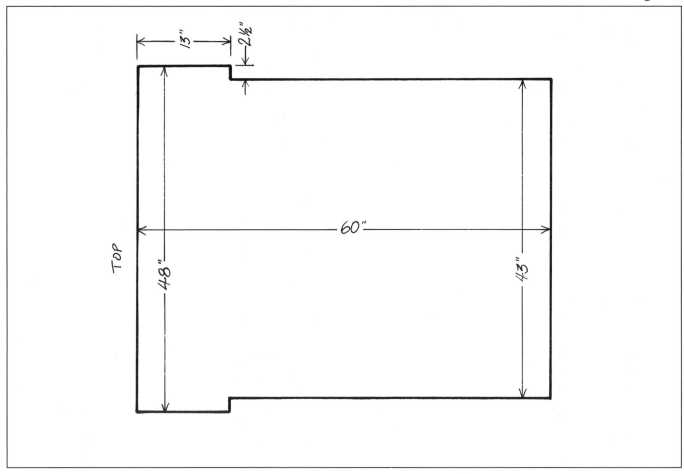

8. Insert the eleven **J** pieces into the holes along the **G** piece of the front section. Join the front and back sections as shown in **Figure H**, using the **A** and **C** pieces as crossbars at the ends and fitting the free ends of the **J** pieces into the holes along the lower **G** piece of the back section.

9. To accommodate the eyebolts, drill a hole straight down through the **M** fitting at each end of both the front and back sections. Drill all the way through, in one side and out the other. Insert the eyebolts from top to bottom and secure each one with a washer and a standard nut.

10. To hang the seat from the frame, attach a length of chain to each eyebolt on the frame. Place the seat inside the frame and attach the free ends of the chains to the eyebolts on the seat. To attach the chain, use the connecting links or the alternate method described in the "Materials" section.

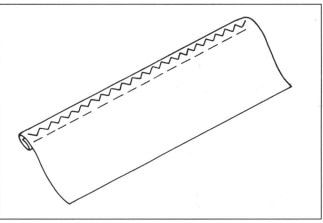

Making the cushion

Note: To avoid shrinkage problems, wash and dry the fabric before cutting the pieces.

1. A cutting diagram for the Front/Back Cushion piece is provided in **Figure I**. You can enlarge the diagram to make a full-size pattern, or simply plot the corner points directly on the fabric and connect them with straight lines. Cut two Front/Back Cushion pieces.

2. The cushion is held in place on the glider by means of a sleeve that fits over the top of the seat back. The sleeve is sewn into the cushion. Cut one Sleeve piece, 13½ x 48 inches. Press a 1-inch-wide hem to the wrong side of the fabric along one long edge, then repeat this procedure on the same edge so that you have a double-turned hem 1 inch wide. Stitch the hem in place. For extra strength, run a line of zigzag stitches along the edge (**Figure J**).

25

Figure K

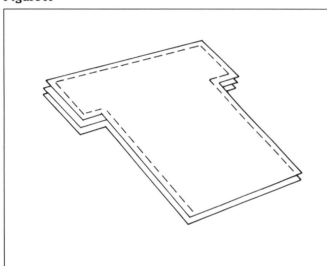

Figure L

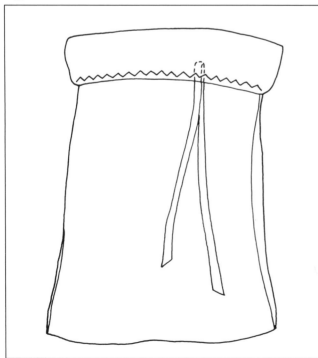

3. Place one Cushion piece right side up on a flat surface. Place the Sleeve piece on top, right side up, aligning the long raw edge of the Sleeve with the top raw edge of the Cushion piece. Place the remaining Cushion piece on top, right side down. Pin the layers together along all edges. Stitch a 1-inch-wide seam along each edge, leaving the bottom edge open and unstitched (**Figure K**). Stitch the seams again for extra strength. If your fabric is ravel-prone, finish all raw edges by zigzagging or pinking.

4. Clip the corners and turn the stitched cushion right side out. Adjust the Sleeve portion so that the wrong side of the fabric lies flat against one side of the cushion. At the lower end of the cushion, press the seam allowances to the inside along the open raw edges. Use the stitched cushion as a pattern to cut as many pieces of quilt batting as you can get out of the two packages of batting. Stack the pieces of batting and tack them together in the center and in several other spots. Insert the batting inside the cushion, easing it into the corners, and then whipstitch the opening edges of the cushion together. For extra strength, you may prefer to machine stitch this closure.

5. The ribbon is used to help secure the cushion to the glider seat. Cut the length of ribbon in half, so you have two 1½-yard lengths. Fold one of these lengths in half and stitch the folded center portion to the wrong side of the cushion Sleeve, close to the free long edge and about 16 inches from one end of the Sleeve (**Figure L**). Fold and attach the remaining length of ribbon in the same manner, 16 inches from the opposite end of the Sleeve.

6. Place the cushion on the glider seat, slipping the Sleeve over the top of the back section. Tie the ends of each ribbon around the pipe at the bottom of the back section.

Making the pillows

1. For each pillow you wish to make, cut two rectangular pieces of fabric, 14 x 18 inches.

2. Pin the pieces right sides together and stitch a 1-inch-wide seam along both long edges and one short edge. Leave the remaining short edge open and unstitched.

3. Clip the corners and turn the stitched pillow right side out. Press the seam allowances to the inside along the open raw edges. Stuff the pillow with fiberfill and then whipstitch the opening edges together.

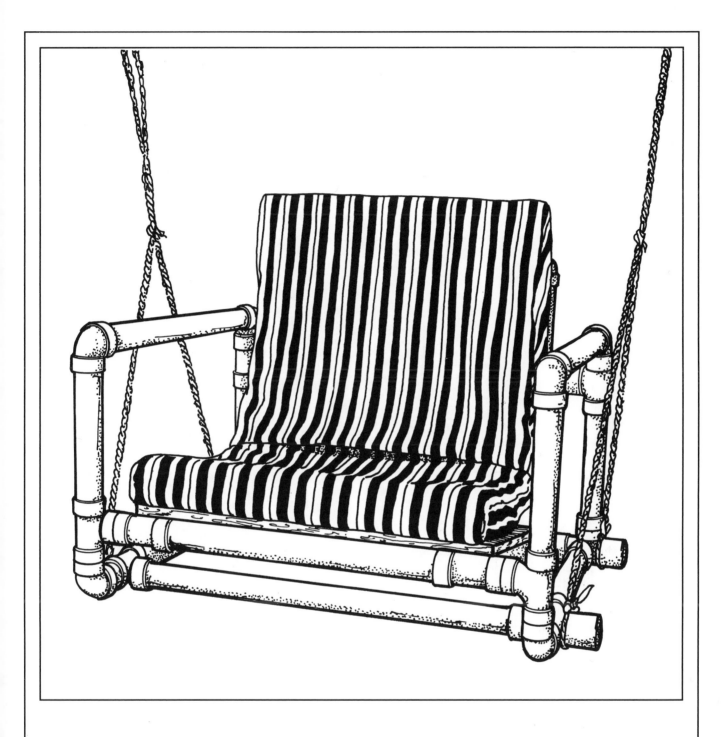

Yard Swing

Kids aren't the only ones who enjoy swinging under the old oak tree. This model is so stylish, you might prefer to hang it on your front porch. It's roomy, too: 34 inches wide, 31 inches deep, and 26 inches tall!

Figure A

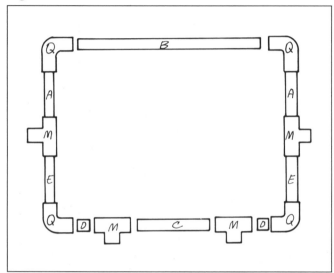

Materials

27 feet of 1½-inch straight PVC pipe.

1½-inch PVC fittings: twelve 90-degree angle joints, fourteen T-joints, four double T-joints, and four end caps.

50 feet of strong rope or chain to hang the swing. We used heavy nylon ski rope, which is both strong and weather resistant. (Be sure that the product you choose is rated to handle well above the weight it will need to hold, or someone may be let down in mid-swing and you could be sued for non-support.)

Cushion: You can use either a one-piece cushion that bends in the middle, or separate cushions for the seat and seat back. (Bed pillows covered with heavy fabric will also work.) The swing will accommodate a cushion between 25 and 28 inches wide. The seat portion is 25 inches long and the seat-back portion, 23½ inches.

PVC solvent cement or 150 No. 6 gauge self-tapping sheet metal screws, each 1 inch long.

Eight weatherproof molly bolts, each long enough to accommodate a "wall" ¾ inch thick.

25 x 46-inch piece of ½-inch exterior-grade plywood or waferwood for the seat and back supports. If you prefer, you can use plastic webbing strips for this purpose and weave them around the swing frame. If you opt for plywood or waferwood, it will need a coat or two of either paint or sealer.

Cutting the pipe

The required lengths of straight pipe listed below were calculated on the basis of ¾-inch fitting allowances. Check the depth of each fitting you purchased and, if necessary, recalculate the pipe lengths to compensate for the difference on each end.

Cut and label the following lengths of pipe.

Part	Length	Quantity
A	7½ inches	2
B	19¼ inches	1
C	11¼ inches	2
D	1⅜ inches	24
E	6 inches	2
F	26 inches	2
G	10¼ inches	4
H	17⅝ inches	2
J	19 inches	1
K	21⅞ inches	2
L	27¾ inches	1

Fittings:

M	T-joint
N	Double T-joint
P	End cap
Q	90-degree joint

Building the frame

The yard swing is assembled in four separate sections: the back section (**Figure A**), two identical side sections (**Figure B**), and the seat section (**Figure C**). The assembled frame is shown in **Figure F**.

1. An assembly diagram of the back section is provided in **Figure A**. The code letters given in the diagram will help you identify the various lengths of straight pipe and the fittings. Begin by assembling the two vertical side portions and the horizontal bottom portion. Be sure that the open ends of the fittings face the directions shown on the diagram. Insert a short **D** piece into the open end of the **Q** fitting at the lower end of each side portion. Then perform the final assembly of the back section, using the long **B** piece at the top.

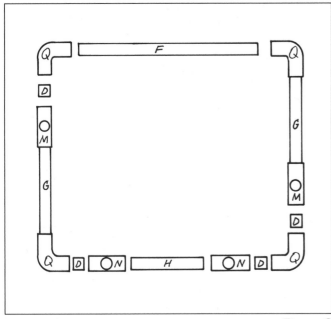

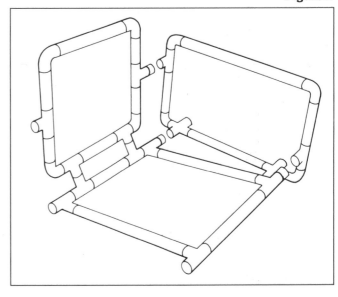

Figure C

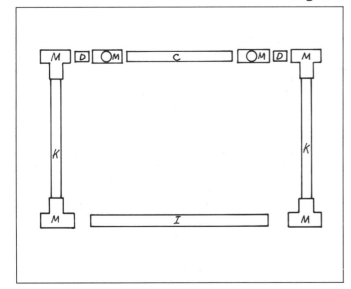

Figure E

2. An assembly diagram of one side section is provided in **Figure B**. You'll need to make two of these, each a mirror image of the other. Assemble each side section as you did the back; first the vertical side portions and the bottom horizontal portion, then the final assembly. Use **D** pieces to connect the fittings where indicated on the diagram, and be sure the open end of each fitting faces the proper direction.

3. An assembly diagram of the seat section is provided in **Figure C**. The **M-C-M** portion (at the top of the diagram) will be the back of the seat section. The open ends of these **M** fittings will be joined to those at the bottom of the section you assembled in step 1. They will have to be tilted at the proper angle, so don't apply any cement or screws to these fittings for the time being.

4. Join the back and seat sections (**Figure D**), using a **D** piece between each of the two **M** fittings.

5. Insert a **D** piece into the open end of each **M** fitting on both sides of the partially assembled swing. Add one side section, adjusting the angle of the back-and-seat assembly so the fittings match (**Figure E**).

Figure H

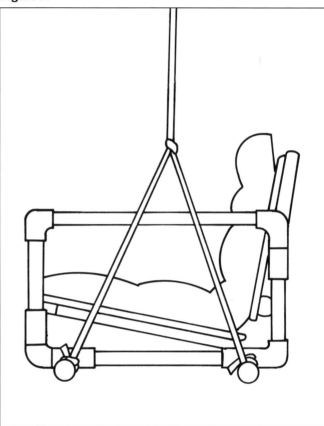

Figure F

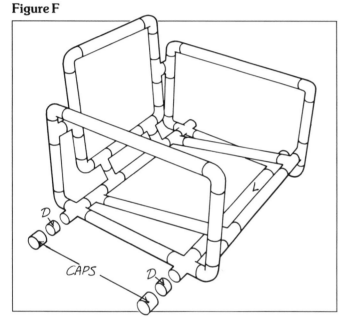

Figure G

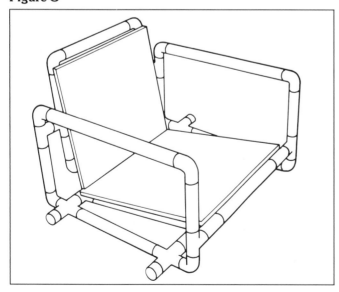

6. Insert the **L** piece into the open fitting on the inside of the attached side section (**Figure F**), and then add the other side section. Use the remaining **D** pieces to attach the caps (**P**) to the **N** fittings on both sides of the swing.

Adding the seat supports

1. Cut the plywood or waferwood into two pieces: a seat support, 25 x 25 inches; and a back support, 23½ x 20½ inches. Sand the edges and apply paint or sealer.

2. Use the molly bolts to attach the supports to the frame (**Figure G**). Place the seat support on the seat section of the frame so that it does not extend past the front crossbar. We used two bolts at the front and two at the back. Place the back support against the back section of the frame and attach it in the same manner.

Hanging the swing

We used a doubled length of rope on each side to hang the swing. It is knotted just above the armrest (the top bar of each side section). The lower ends of each rope are securely tied around the capped fittings that extend beyond the side of the swing (**Figure H**). Tie the ends loosely, then hang the swing and adjust the ropes before tightening the knots. (If your knotting knowledge is not up to snuff, consult a local boy scout, sailor, or library.)

Picnic Table

You might as well invite the ants...they'll come anyway! But instead of giving those ground-level gourmets an easy target, elevate your friends, family, and food on this spiffy picnic table. It features a redwood tabletop, 40 x 60 inches, benches and backrests.

Figure A

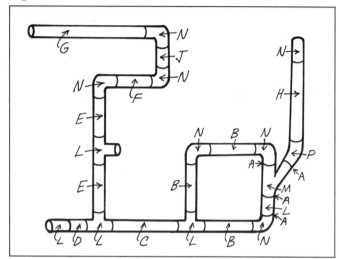

Figure B

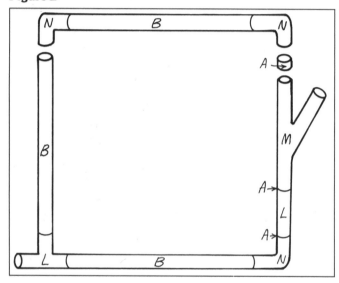

Figure C

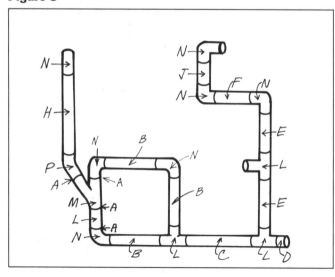

Materials

65 feet of 1½-inch straight PVC pipe.

1½-inch PVC fittings: eighteen T-joints, four Y-joints, twenty-eight 90-degree angle joints, and four 45-degree angle joints.

45 linear feet of 2 x 8-inch redwood. The redwood will be used in 5-foot lengths.

PVC solvent cement; or a multitude of No. 6 gauge self-tapping sheet metal screws, each 1 inch long.

A large handful of 2½-inch-long wood screws, for attaching the wooden parts to the PVC frame.

Clear polyurethane to seal the wood.

Cutting the pipe

The lengths of straight pipe listed below were calculated on the basis of ¾-inch fitting allowances. Check the depth of the fittings you purchased and, if necessary, recalculate the lengths of pipe to compensate for the difference on each end. Cut and label the pieces of straight pipe. Label the fittings as listed below.

Part	Length	Quantity
A	1⅜ inches	20
B	10 inches	12
C	13 inches	4
D	3½ inches	4
E	6½ inches	8
F	7 inches	4
G	27¾ inches	2
H	16 inches	4
J	4 inches	4
K	48 inches	7

Fittings:

L	T-joint
M	Y-joint
N	90-degree joint
P	45-degree joint

Assembly

The PVC frame consists of two pairs of nearly identical sections (**Figures A** and **C**) that are mirror images of one another. The sections are joined together in two pairs (**Figure D**), each pair forming one end of the table-and-bench frame. In the final step, the two end assemblies are joined by long connecting bars (**Figure E**). The code letters which appear on the assembly diagrams will help you identify the various lengths of straight pipe and the fittings.

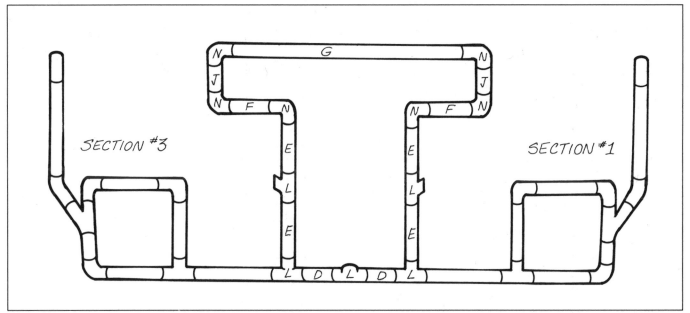

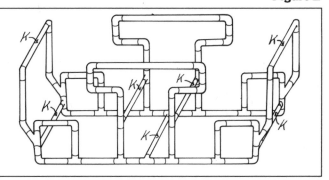

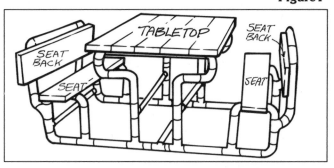

One assembled frame section is shown in **Figure A**. An explanation of what you're looking at here is probably in order, since it makes the assembly process less mystifying. The long **G** piece at the upper left will support one end of the wooden tabletop. (The free end of the **G** piece will connect to another section that's a mirror image of the one you're building.) The closed rectangular assembly at the lower right is the bench support; the **B** piece at the top of this rectangle will support one end of the seat board. The assembly that periscopes up to the right from this rectangle is the seat-back support. In the final assembly, a long connecting pipe will be inserted into each open fitting.

1. There's only one tricky part to assembling the frame section – the closed rectangle – and that's the best place to begin. Assemble the vertical right side of the rectangle, then continue around the bottom portion and up the left side (**Figure B**). Assemble the top portion separately, and then install it as shown. From there on it's clear sailing – just add the pipe and fittings, one at a time, as shown in **Figure A**. Be sure that any fitting with an open end is facing the proper direction.

2. Assemble another section exactly the same as the first one. When the final assembly is performed, this section will go diagonally opposite the first section – at the opposite end of the table and on the opposite side.

3. Assemble a third section, making it a mirror image of the first two but leaving off two pieces: the long **G** piece at the top, and the **L** fitting at the open end of the lower portion. The third section is shown in **Figure C**.

4. Assemble a fourth section, exactly the same as the third one (**Figure C**).

5. To make one complete end pair, join the first and third sections as shown in **Figure D**. Join the remaining two sections in the same manner.

6. Use the long **K** pieces to connect the two end assemblies, as shown in **Figure E**.

Adding the wooden parts

1. Cut the redwood into nine equal boards, each 5 feet long. Sand the edges smooth.

2. Attach the boards to the PVC frame as shown in **Figure F**, using two wood screws at each end of each board. We inserted the screws through the pipe first, and into the undersides of the boards. Use one board for each seat, one for each seat back, and the remaining five for the tabletop.

3. Seal all of the boards, using polyurethane, and allow them to dry thoroughly before you light the charcoal.

Parson's Table

This sturdy little table will find many uses in your home, and you can put it together in an afternoon. We stained the 17-inch-square top in a checkerboard pattern, so it can be used as a game table. And it's just the right height, 17 inches, to use as an occasional end table.

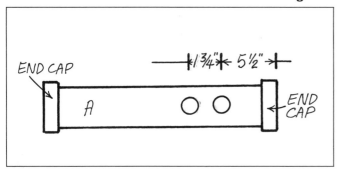

Materials

5½ feet of 2-inch straight PVC pipe.

6 feet of ¾-inch straight CPVC pipe.

2-inch PVC fittings: eight end caps.

PVC solvent cement, or sixteen self-tapping sheet metal screws, each 1 inch long.

Eight self-tapping sheet metal screws, each ⅝ inch long.

17 x 26-inch piece of ⅜-inch lumber-core plywood. We used baltic birch, but any plywood with a nice finish will do.

Twenty-five 2d finishing nails.

Ten-inch length of 1½-inch closet rod for the checkers.

Wood filler, stain or paint, and wood glue.

Assembling the frame

This simple PVC frame consists of two basically identical sections (**Figure B**), that are assembled in an x-shape. The assembled frame is shown in **Figure C**.

1. The lengths of 2-inch straight pipe listed below were calculated on the basis of ½-inch fitting allowances. The height of the table may vary slightly if the end caps you purchased have a different fitting allowance. You don't need to recalculate the lengths as long as all of the caps have the *same* fitting allowance. Keep in mind that all four legs must be the same length or the table will wobble. Cut and label the pieces of pipe listed below.

Part	Length	Quantity
A	15 inches	4

2. Cut and label the pieces of ¾-inch straight pipe listed below. Do not recalculate for fitting allowances.

Part	Length	Quantity
B	17½ inches	4

3. One leg is shown in **Figure A**. First, install the two end

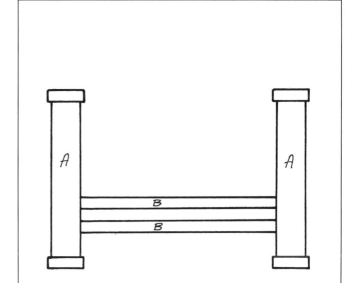

caps. Drill a 1-inch diameter hole into the straight pipe, 5½ inches from the bottom end. Drill through one side of the pipe only. Do not continue to drill through the opposite side. Drill another hole 1¾ inches above the first one.

4. Assemble and drill an identical second leg.

5. Assemble the third leg in the same manner. This time, drill a 1-inch hole 4½ inches from the bottom end. Then drill another hole 1¾ inches above the first one.

6. Assemble and drill a fourth leg identical to the third one.

7. One assembled frame section is shown in **Figure B**. Assemble one section, using two of the **B** pieces to join the first two legs you made.

Figure C

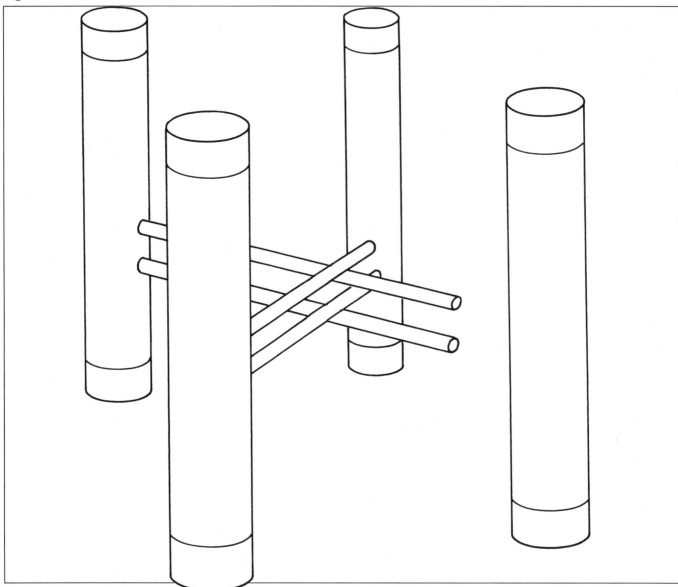

Figure D

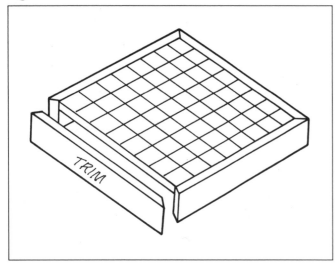

TRIM

8. Insert the remaining two **B** pieces into the holes in the third leg. Slide the two frame sections together, forming an x with the crossbars (**Figure C**). The upper crossbar slides between the two crossbars of the assembled frame section. Finally, insert the open ends of the crossbars into the fourth leg.

Making the top

1. Cut the following pieces from plywood.

Dimensions	Quantity
16 x 16 inches	1
16¾ x 2 inches	4

2. Miter both ends of each narrow piece so they will fit together at the corners (**Figure D**).

3. Glue and nail the mitered trim pieces to the edges of the top piece as shown in **Figure D**.

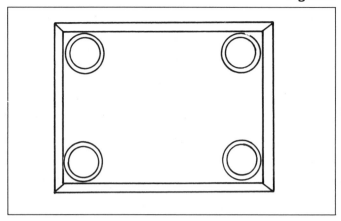

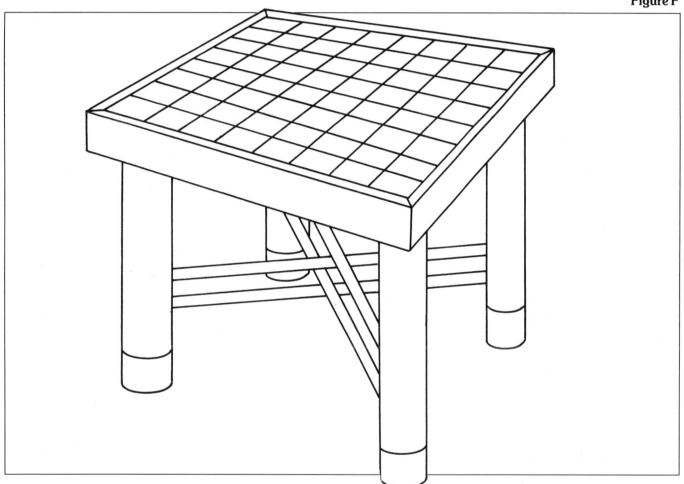

4. Place the assembled top over the pipe frame, and mark the positions of the upper end caps on the underside of the wooden top. Remove the tabletop from the frame, and remove the upper end caps from the legs. Glue one end cap underneath each corner of the assembled top (**Figure E**), aligned with your pencil marks. If you're going to do a lot of table thumping, you can increase the strength of the bond by countersinking a ⅝-inch screw from inside each cap to the top trim pieces it touches.

Final assembly

To make the checkerboard pattern, pencil a grid of 2-inch squares, eight on a side, on the wooden top. Stain or paint every other square. Install the top on the pipe frame (**Figure F**). To make checkers, cut twenty-four ⅜-inch-thick slices from the 1½-inch closet rod. Stain or paint half of them.

Hammock

Put the lemonade in the refrigerator and by the time it's good and cold you can build this PVC hammock stand. Overall dimensions are 138 x 37 x 36 inches. The heavy cotton hammock takes only a few hours to stitch up. The structure is self-supporting so the only thing you need a tree for is the shade.

Materials

For the stand:

50 feet of straight 2½-inch PVC pipe.

2½-inch PVC fittings: fourteen 45-degree angle joints; twelve Y-joints; four T-joints; and four end caps.

16 feet of straight 1½-inch PVC pipe.

PVC solvent cement or a handful of No. 6 gauge self-tapping sheet metal screws, each 1 inch long.

Two 5-foot lengths of No. 8 chain.

Six connecting links, each one size larger than the chain. (You can eliminate the connecting links if you're strong enough to pry open the eyebolts to insert the chain.)

Four 4-inch-long eyebolts, each with two washers and a standard nut; and two 6-inch-long eyebolts, each with three washers and a standard nut.

Two 1½-inch-diameter wooden macrame balls. (A macrame ball is a sphere with a hole drilled through the center.)

For the hammock:

3½ yards of heavy cotton fabric (duck or canvas), 60 inches wide. We used a red-white-and-blue-striped fabric.

One standard-size bed pillow.

Heavy-duty thread to match the fabric.

Building the stand

The hammock stand consists of six sections and six connecting bars. A yoke section (**Figure A**) is joined to two corner sections (**Figure B**) and a crossbar to form each end of the stand (**Figure C**). The two end assemblies are then joined by long connecting bars to form the complete stand (**Figure D**).

1. The required lengths of 2½-inch straight pipe listed below were calculated on the basis of ¾-inch fitting allowances. Check the depth of each fitting and, if necessary, recalculate the length of each straight piece of pipe to compensate for the difference on each end. Cut and label the straight pieces of pipe listed below. Label the fittings as listed.

Part	Length	Quantity
A	1⅜ inches	16
B	23 inches	4
C	9½ inches	4
D	9¼ inches	4
E	5 inches	4
F	26 inches	2
G	60 inches	2
H	68¼ inches	2
J	36 inches	2
Fittings:		
K	Y-joint	
L	T-joint	
M	End cap	
N	45-degree joint	

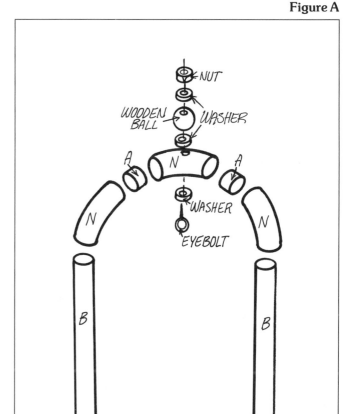

Figure A

2. Refer to **Figure A** as you assemble the pipe and fittings to form one yoke section. The short **A** pieces will be covered completely by the fittings they join.

3. The hammock will hang from an eyebolt inserted through the top of each yoke. Drill a hole straight down through the uppermost **N** fitting, in one side and out the other. Use a bit that is slightly larger in diameter than the 6-inch eyebolt shank. Place a washer on the eyebolt, insert the bolt through the hole from the bottom up, then install another washer, a wooden macrame ball, and a third washer. Fasten the assembly with a nut.

Figure B

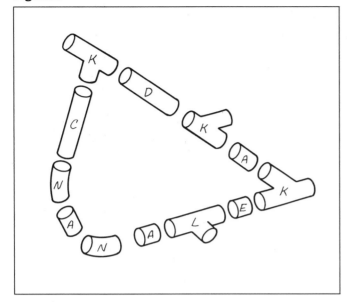

Figure C

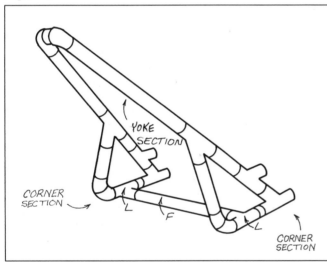

YOKE
SECTION

CORNER
SECTION

L   F   L

CORNER
SECTION

Figure D

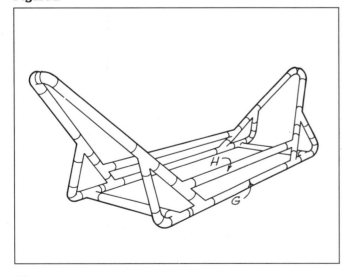

H

G

Figure E

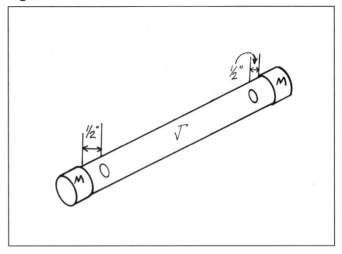

½"   ½"

J

M   M

4. Make a second yoke section, repeating the procedures in steps 2 and 3.

5. Refer to **Figure B** as you assemble one corner section. Start with the bottom **K** fitting and assemble the parts in the order shown. The open end of the **L** fitting should face what will be the center of the hammock. Be sure the open end of the **K** fitting in the center of the upper arm is pointing in the direction shown. The top **K** fitting joins the two arms; slip it over the arm ends to complete the section.

6. Repeat the procedures in step 5 to assemble three more corner sections. When finished, the two corner sections for one side of the hammock should be mirror images of the two for the opposite side, with the open end of each **L** fitting facing the center of the stand.

7. Now assemble one complete end of the stand (**Figure C**). Insert a straight **F** piece into the open **L** fitting in one corner section. Add the second corner section. Cut the 1½-inch PVC pipe into four 4-foot lengths. Insert one of these pieces into the top **K** fitting of each corner section, and slide it down to the bottom. Then install the assembled yoke section on top, sliding it down over the 1½-inch-pipe reinforcing pieces.

8. Repeat the procedures in step 7 to assemble the opposite end of the stand.

9. Don't break out the lemonade just yet, but make sure it's getting cold. Connect the two assembled ends, using a **G** and an **H** piece at each side (**Figure D**).

10. The **J** pieces will support the ends of the fabric hammock. Install an end cap (**M**) on each end of one **J** piece. Drill a hole straight down through the pipe, in one side and out the other, placing the center of the hole ½ inch from the end cap (**Figure E**). Use a bit that is slightly larger in diameter than the 4-inch eyebolt shank. Slip a washer onto the eyebolt, insert the bolt through the hole, add another washer, and secure it with a nut. Drill a hole through the pipe near the opposite end in the same manner, making sure that it is drilled along the same axis as the first hole. Install an eyebolt, with washers and nut.

11. Repeat the procedures in step 10 using the remaining **J** piece, **M** fittings, and eyebolts.

HAMMOCK 30" x 87"	PILLOW 20" x 30"	
		POCKET 10½" x 15"
HAMMOCK 30" x 87"	PILLOW 20" x 30"	ORGANIZER 15" x 16½"
		ORGANIZER 15" x 16½"

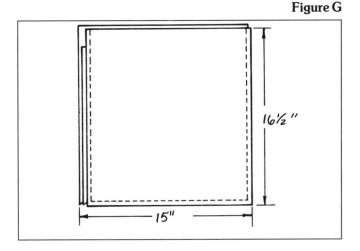

Making the hammock

The fabric hammock is a large, double-layered rectangle with a casing at each end to accommodate the pipe support. We made a simple organizer that is sewn into one of the side seams. It hangs from the hammock, and will hold magazines, eyeglasses, writing paper, and other necessities of lazy living. The pillow is covered in the same fabric, but is not attached to the hammock.

1. All of the required fabric pieces are listed below. A cutting diagram is provided in **Figure F**.

Hammock, 30 x 87 inches – cut two
Organizer, 15 x 16½ inches – cut two
Pocket, 10½ x 15 inches – cut one
Pillow, 20 x 30 inches – cut two

2. Stitch up the organizer first, so it can be sewn into a side seam of the hammock body. On the Pocket piece, press a ½-inch-wide hem to the wrong side of the fabric along one long edge only. Machine stitch the hem.

3. Place one Organizer piece right side up on a flat surface. Place the Pocket piece on top, right side up, aligning the unhemmed long edge of the Pocket piece with one 15-inch edge of the Organizer piece. Place the remaining Organizer piece on top, right side down, and pin the layers together along each edge. Stitch a ½-inch-wide seam along the three edges that include the Pocket piece, leaving the remaining edge open and unstitched (**Figure G**).

4. Clip the corners, turn the stitched organizer right side out, and press. Baste the open edges together, ¼ inch from the raw edges.

5. Place one Hammock piece right side up on a flat surface. Place the organizer on top, aligning the basted edge with one side edge of the Hammock piece. You can place the organizer equally distant from each end, or closer to one end than the other for easy reaching. Place the remaining Hammock piece on top, right side down, and pin the layers together along each edge.

41

Figure H

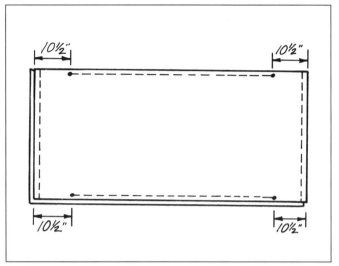

Figure I

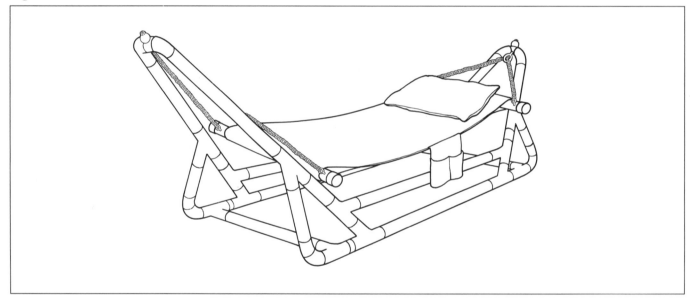

6. Stitch a ½-inch-wide seam along each short edge. Stitch a ½-inch-wide seam along each long edge, leaving a 10½-inch space open and unstitched at each end (**Figure H**). The openings will form the casings for the pipe supports. Press the seams open.

7. Turn the hammock right side out. Press the seam allowances to the inside along the open portions of each side seam. Machine stitch these allowances in place.

8. To make the pillow cover, pin the two Pillow pieces right sides together. Stitch a ½-inch-wide seam along each long edge and one short edge, leaving the remaining short edge open. Clip the corners and press the seams open. (To make a removable cover, simply hem the open edges.)

9. Turn the stitched pillow cover right side out and press

the seam allowances to the inside along the open edges. Insert the pillow and stitch the open edges together.

Final assembly

1. Find the **J** pieces with end caps and eyebolts that you assembled in steps 10 and 11 of "Building the stand." Insert one of these through the casing at one end of the fabric hammock. Insert the other through the casing at the opposite end.

2. The hammock is attached to the stand with a 5-foot length of chain at each end (**Figure I**). Use a connecting link to attach each end of each chain to an eyebolt, as shown. Use an additional connecting link to attach the center link of each chain to the eyebolt at one end of the hammock stand.

3. Find some shade and pour the lemonade.

Etagere

At 16 x 29 x 71 inches, this etagere will hold a wealth of knickknacks.

Figure A

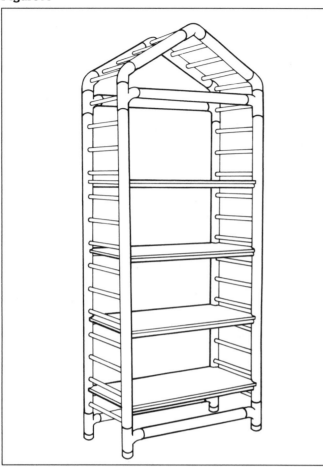

Figure B

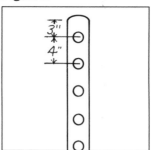

Figure C

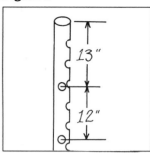

Materials

67 feet of ¾-inch straight CPVC pipe.

32 feet of 1½-inch straight PVC pipe.

1½-inch PVC fittings: four end caps, eight T-joints, and six 60-degree angle joints.

PVC and CPVC solvent cement; or a large handful of No. 6 gauge self-tapping sheet metal screws, each ½ inch long.

Sixteen No. 6 gauge self-tapping sheet metal screws, each 1 inch long (optional). These can be used to secure the plywood shelves to the PVC frame, but they're not really necessary unless you intend to use your etagere upside-down, perhaps as a piece of modern art.

4 x 4-foot sheet of ½-inch-thick plywood or waferwood for the shelves.

Cutting and drilling the pipe

The required lengths of straight pipe listed below were calculated on the basis of ¾-inch-long fitting allowances. Check the depth of each fitting. If the straight pipe can be inserted more or less than ¾ inch, recalculate the length of each straight piece of pipe to compensate for the difference on each end.

1. The assembled etagere is shown in **Figure A**. It has identical front and back frames (**Figure D**) made from 1½-inch

PVC pipe and fittings. The shelf supports on each frame are straight lengths of ¾-inch CPVC pipe. The two frames are connected by side rails that are also cut from ¾-inch CPVC pipe. Begin by cutting and labeling the following straight pieces of 1½-inch PVC pipe. Label the fittings as listed.

Part	Length	Quantity
A	52½ inches	4
B	13⅞ inches	4
C	2 feet	4
D	1½ inches	8
Fittings:		
E	T-joint	
F	60-degree joint	
G	End cap	

2. Cut the following straight pieces from ¾-inch CPVC pipe. It is not necessary to recalculate to compensate for fitting allowances.

Part	Length	Quantity
H	15¼ inches	37
J	28¾ inches	8

3. You'll need to drill 1-inch-diameter holes into the four corner posts (**A**) to accommodate the shelf supports (**J**) and the side rails (**H**). The holes for the side rails are spaced at 4-inch intervals, measured center to center (**Figure B**). Drill thirteen holes in each corner post, paying special attention to the alignment. First draw a straight center line down one "side" of one post. Drill the first hole, centered on the line, 3 inches from one end of the pipe. (This will be the top.) Drill twelve more holes below the first one, keeping the line as straight as possible. Drill thirteen holes in each corner post in this manner.

4. Now drill four additional holes in each corner post to accommodate the shelf supports. These holes should also be drilled in a straight vertical line, one-quarter of the way around the post from the existing line of holes (**Figure C**). Pay special attention to the placement of this line of holes because all four posts should be mirror images of each other (**Figure A**). We placed the holes at 12-inch intervals beginning 13 inches from the top of the post (**Figure C**), but you may prefer to vary the spacing if you want shelves of different heights. Just be sure to measure carefully so that the holes are aligned on all four posts.

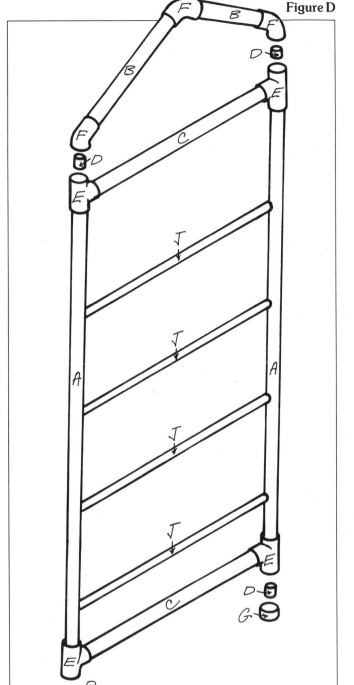

Figure D

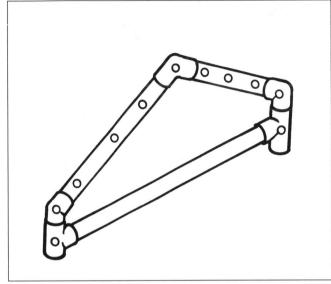

Figure E

Assembling the Frame

A diagram of the identical front and back frames is provided in **Figure D**. The code letters on the diagram will help you to identify the various pieces. Each frame is dry assembled in three sections: the upper section includes the top horizontal (**C**) piece and the peak assembly; the middle section includes two corner posts (**A**) and four shelf supports (**J**); the lower section includes the remaining pieces that form the base.

1. To assemble the upper section of one frame, begin by inserting each end of one **C** piece into an **E** fitting. Make the peak assembly by joining two **B** pieces and three **F** fittings as shown. Now attach the peak to the **E-C-E** assembly by inserting one **D** piece between each **E** and **F**. (When the joints are fitted together, the **D** pieces will not show. They will be covered completely by the **E**'s and **F**'s.)

2. Insert four shelf supports (**J**) between two corner posts (**A**), using the four aligned holes in each post.

3. To make the bottom section, insert one **C** piece between two **E** fittings. Use a short **D** piece to join one **G** fitting to the bottom of each **E** fitting. Be sure that the open ends of the fittings face the proper direction.

4. Complete the frame assembly by inserting the upper ends of the middle-section corner posts into the **E** fittings of the upper section, and the lower ends of the posts into the **E** fittings of the lower section.

5. Repeat the procedures in steps 1 through 4 to assemble a second, identical frame.

6. Before you connect the front and back frames, you have a little more drilling to do. As you can see in **Figure A**, the upper sections of the front and back frames are joined by side rails in the same manner that the corner posts are. **Figure E** shows placement of the eleven holes you're about to drill into the upper section of each frame. Begin by drilling a hole into the center of the **F** fitting at the top of the peak. (Be sure to drill all of these holes on the same side of the frame as the line of thirteen holes for the side rails.) Drill three holes into the **B** piece on each side of the **F**, at 4-inch intervals. Drill one hole into the **F** fitting at the lower end of each **B** piece as shown, 4 inches from the last hole. Drill one hole into each **E** fitting, just above the lower cuff. Drill both frames in this manner.

Figure F

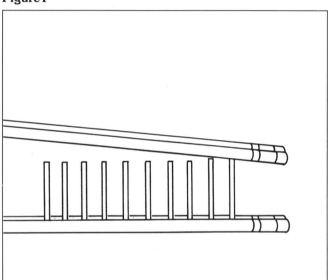

Figure G

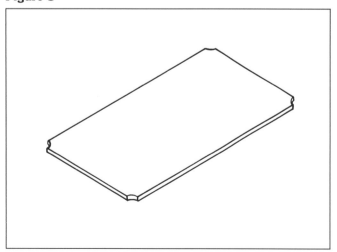

7. Now stand back and survey both frames. Check to be sure that everything matches up properly and looks level, even, and square (unless you prefer it to look wacky, unprofessional, or artistic, depending on your point of view and what you had for breakfast). Secure the main joints of each frame using either pipe cement or short self-tapping screws.

8. To connect the front and back frames, place one of them flat on the floor or on a table, with the holes for the side rails facing upward. Insert the side rails (**H**) into the holes.

9. Place the remaining frame on top with the holes facing downward (**Figure F**). Guide the free ends of the side rails into the holes, starting at the bottom and working side to side. Tap the top frame, using a soft mallet, until the spacing between the frames is even all the way around. We did not use cement or screws to secure the side rails, but you may wish to do so. Securing at least some of the rails will prevent your accidentally pulling the front and back frames apart, which we sincerely hope will not happen when you're moving the assembled structure, fully loaded (the etagere, not you).

Adding the Shelves

1. Cut four shelves from plywood or waferwood, each 15 x 28¼ inches.

2. The corners of the shelves must be cut out so they will fit snugly around the corner posts. Mark a 1-inch-radius quarter circle on all four corners of one shelf, using a compass or a string and a pencil. Cut out the corners (**Figure G**) and sand the edges, then place the shelf in the assembled frame to test for fit. The long front and back edges of the shelf should rest on aligned front and back shelf support pieces. It may be necessary to increase the size of the corner cutouts, but it's best to start small since an over-large cutout will look sloppy. Repeat these procedures for the remaining shelves.

3. The shelves can be attached to the supports using self-tapping screws, or they may be left loose since there's very little chance of one falling off.

Playhouse

This playhouse is nearly 4 feet square and 60 inches tall at the peak of the roof.

Figure A

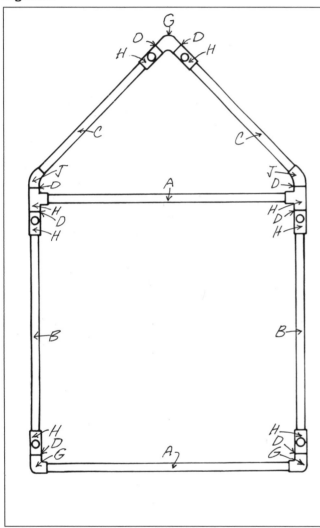

Materials

For the frame:

61 feet of 1¼-inch straight PVC pipe.

20 feet of ¾-inch straight CPVC pipe.

1¼-inch PVC fittings: six 90-degree angle joints, sixteen T-joints, and four 45-degree angle joints.

PVC solvent cement or approximately seventy No. 6 gauge self-tapping sheet metal screws, each ½ or ¾ inch long.

For the cover:

8¼ yards of 60-inch-wide white polyester double-knit fabric for the walls. We used polyester double-knit because it will not ravel, so you won't have to hem all of the edges.

2½ yards of 60-inch-wide red polyester double-knit fabric for the roof and trim. You may wish to substitute a "cooler" color, but it should be one that contrasts nicely with the white walls.

1 yard of dark blue fabric for the window shutters. We used a lightweight fleece, but you may use whatever fabric you have on hand.

2¾ yards of 36-inch-wide red-and-white striped fabric for the window curtains.

3 yards of ½-inch-wide red braid trim.

1-foot length of 1-inch-wide white eyelet trim.

3½ yards of 1¼-inch-wide red ribbon, and 2½ yards of green. We used the type with scallop trim along the edges. If you choose a color other than red for the roof, you may wish to substitute a matching color for the red ribbon.

Five 5-inch squares of yellow felt for the flower blossoms.

Wooden dowel rod: Two 3-foot lengths of ⅜-inch-diameter, and one 2-foot length of ¼- or ⅜-inch-diameter.

Heavy-duty white thread.

Cutting the pipe

The lengths of straight pipe listed below were calculated on the basis of 1-inch-long fitting allowances. Check the depth of each fitting and, if necessary, recalculate the lengths of pipe to compensate for the difference on each end.

1. Cut and label the lengths of 1¼-inch PVC pipe. Label the fittings as listed.

Part	Length	Quantity
A	43¾ inches	10
B	34¾ inches	4
C	26½ inches	4
D	2 inches	16

Fittings:

G	90-degree joint	
H	T-joint	
J	45-degree joint	

2. The CPVC pipe is cut into five lengths that will serve as roof supports. These pieces will be inserted into holes drilled in the PVC pipe and fittings, so it is not necessary to recalculate the lengths to compensate for fitting allowances. Cut the following pieces from CPVC pipe:

Part	Length	Quantity
E	46¼ inches	3
F	47 inches	2

Building the frame

The pipe frame consists of two identical sections (**Figure A**) that are connected by crossbars and roof supports in the final assembly (**Figure E**). Each section consists of a rectangular lower portion and a triangular upper portion that supports the roof. One assembled section is shown in **Figure A**.

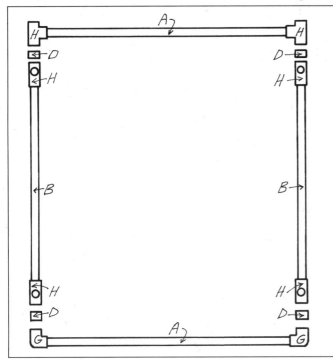

Figure B

Figure C

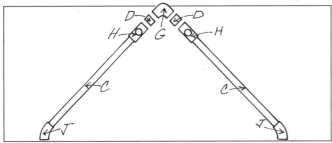

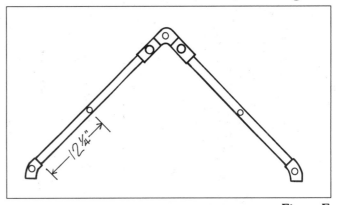

Figure D

Figure E

1. Construct the lower rectangular portion of one section, as shown in **Figure B**. The code letters given with the diagram will help you identify the various lengths of straight pipe and the fittings. Begin by assembling the two vertical side portions, making sure the open ends of the fittings are turned in the proper direction, and then connect the two sides using the **A** pieces. The short **D** pieces will not show when the assembly is complete.

2. Construct the upper triangular portion of one section as shown in **Figure C**.

3. Join the upper and lower portions as shown in **Figure A**, using a short **D** piece to connect the **J** and **H** fittings on each side.

4. Repeat steps 1, 2, and 3 to make an identical section.

5. Five holes are drilled in the upper portion of each section to accommodate the CPVC roof supports. Place one assembled section flat on a work surface so that the open ends of the fittings face upward. Drill five holes, each 1 inch in diameter, where indicated in **Figure D**. Drill each hole through one side of the pipe or fitting only, not completely through and out the other side. Drill identically placed holes in the other assembled section.

6. The final assembly is quite simple, but it can be awkward if you don't have an extra pair of hands to assist you. (We used to have great success in luring one or more of the kids into the workshop by making vague references to fortune and fame, but they're getting wise to this ruse and now demand money up front.) The completed frame is shown in **Figure E**. Stand one of the completed sections in an upright position or prop it up against a wall, and insert the crossbars and roof supports in the following manner: Insert one of the remaining **A** pieces of pipe into each of the open **H** fittings. Insert one of the **E** pieces of pipe into the hole you drilled in the **G** fitting at the top of the peak. Insert one of the remaining **E** pieces into the hole in each of the **J** fittings. Insert one of the **F** pieces of pipe into the hole in each of the **C** pieces.

7. Fit the remaining assembled section onto the free ends of the crossbars and roof supports.

49

Figure F

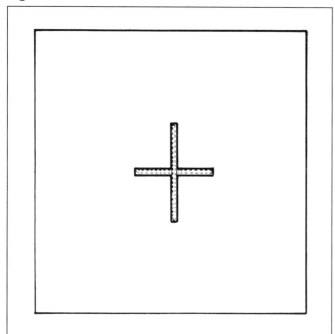

Figure G

Figure H

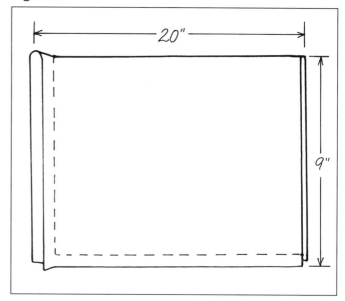

Figure I

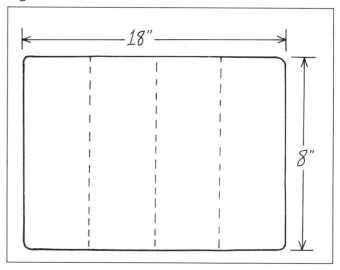

Making the cover

1. Cut two 50-inch squares of white polyester fabric for the Side Walls.

2. We made a window in one of the Side Walls. The window border and pane dividers are made of red ribbon. Cut one 14-inch length and one 17-inch length of red ribbon. Pin them to the center of one Side Wall, on the right side of the fabric, crossed in the middle as shown in **Figure F**. Stitch them in place, by hand or machine. Cut a 2-yard length of red ribbon for the window border. Pin it to the Side Wall (**Figure G**) so that it covers the ends of the ribbon pane dividers, folding it neatly at each corner. Stitch it in place and cut out the white fabric inside the border of each window pane.

3. The window has two shutters, one on each side. Cut two Shutter pieces from dark blue fabric, each 18 x 20 inches. Fold one Shutter piece in half widthwise, placing right sides together. (You should now have a rectangle measuring 9 x 20 inches.) Stitch a 1-inch-wide seam along one short edge and the long edge, leaving the remaining short edge open and unstitched (**Figure H**). Clip the corners, turn the stitched shutter right side out, and press the seam allowances to the inside along the open raw edges. Whipstitch the opening edges together. Run three or four evenly spaced lines of topstitching through both thicknesses, from side to side (**Figure I**). Follow the same procedures to make another shutter, using the remaining Shutter piece.

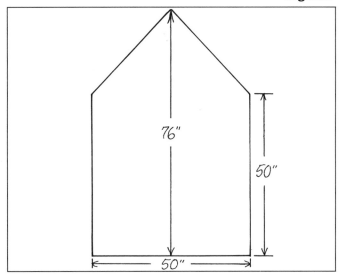

76"

50"

50"

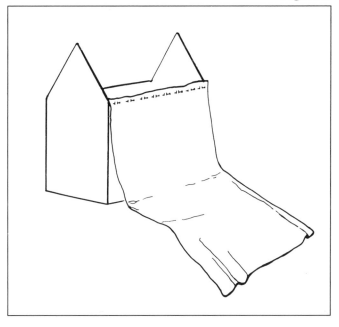

Figure L

4. Pin the shutters to the right side of the Side Wall, one at either side of the window. Whipstitch them in place.

5. A cutting diagram of the Front/Back Wall is provided in **Figure J**. You can either enlarge the diagram to make a full-size pattern, or take the easy way out. We prefer the easy way. To do this, work directly from the diagram, plotting the crucial points (top of roof peak, and top and bottom of each vertical side) directly on the white polyester fabric, and connecting the points with straight lines. Cut one Front Wall and one Back Wall.

6. Pin the Front Wall and one Side Wall right sides together along one side edge, and stitch a 1-inch-wide seam (**Figure K**). Press the seam open. Stitch the remaining Side Wall to the opposite edge of the Front Wall in the same manner.

7. Pin and stitch the Back Wall to the opposite edge of one Side Wall in the same manner. Then fold the entire assembly right sides together to stitch the opposite edge of the Back Wall to the free Side Wall, to complete the basic box.

8. Cut a 73 x 60-inch piece of red polyester fabric for the Roof. Pin one 60-inch edge of the Roof piece along the upper edge of one Side Wall, placing right sides together and leaving equal extensions of the Roof piece on each side of the Wall (**Figure L**). Stitch the seam. Turn the walls inside out, and stitch the opposite end of the Roof piece to the upper edge of the opposite Side Wall in the same manner. There's a lot of fabric involved, so be sure that the pieces are not tangled or twisted before you stitch the second seam.

9. Turn the entire assembly right side out and slip it down over the playhouse frame. Pin the apex of the Front Wall piece to the center front edge of the Roof piece, and do the same at the back. Adjust the pins so that the front and back edges of the Roof piece hang over the Front and Back Walls evenly. Hand stitch the upper edges of the Front Wall to the wrong side of the Roof piece, so that the Roof piece overhangs the wall evenly. Repeat this procedure to attach the upper edges of the Back Wall to the Roof piece. Cut the roof overhang into a scallop design at both the front and back.

10. To "hem" the playhouse cover, simply trim the lower edge wherever it drags the ground.

Making the front door and trim

1. Cut a front door opening in the Front Wall, 19 inches wide and 39 inches tall. To make the door flap, cut a piece of white polyester fabric 40 x 41 inches. Fold the fabric in half widthwise, placing right sides together. (You should now have a rectangle 20 x 41 inches.) Stitch a 1-inch-wide seam along one short edge and the long edge, leaving the remaining short edge open and unstitched. Turn the stitched door flap right side out and press. Machine baste the open raw edges together.

Figure M

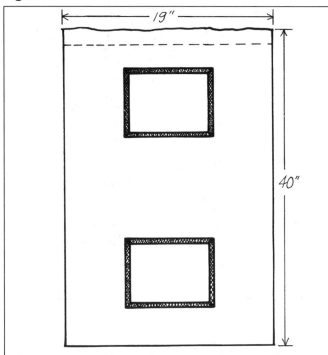

Figure N

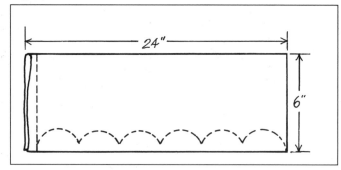

Figure O

2. We used red braid trim to decorate the door flap. Make two separate rectangular outlines of braid on one side of the flap, folding the braid neatly at each corner and stitching it in place (**Figure M**). Pin the basted raw edges of the door flap to the wrong side of the Front Wall, just above the top of the door opening. Hand stitch the door flap in place. We used a 21-inch length of red braid trim to secure the bottom of the door opening. Stitch one end of the braid to the wrong side of the Front Wall, at the bottom of door opening on one side. Stitch the opposite end of the trim to the other lower corner of the door opening.

3. To keep the sides of the door opening from sagging, we strengthened them with fabric-covered dowel rods. Use the two 3-foot lengths of ⅜-inch dowel for this. To cover each dowel, cut a 3 x 38-inch piece of red polyester fabric. Fold the fabric in half lengthwise, placing wrong sides together. Stitch a ¾-inch-wide seam along one short edge and the long edge, leaving the remaining short edge open. Insert the dowel rod inside the tube and stitch across the open end. Pin the covered rod along one vertical side of the door opening, placing the long seamed edges of the red fabric against the wrong side of the wall fabric, and hand stitch. Repeat these procedures for the other side of the door opening.

4. We made a scalloped trim piece to go over the front door. Cut a 12 x 24-inch piece of red polyester fabric. Fold it in half lengthwise, placing right sides together. (You should now have a 6 x 24-inch rectangle.) Stitch a 1-inch-wide seam along one short edge. On the long edge, stitch a scalloped seam (**Figure N**), leaving the remaining short edge open and unstitched. Clip the curves and corners, and turn the piece right side out. Press the seam allowances to the inside along the opening edges and whipstitch them together. Pin the assembled trim piece to the right side of the front wall above

the door opening, so the scalloped edge covers the top of the opening. Hand stitch the trim in place.

5. To make the flower box, cut an 8 x 13-inch piece of red polyester fabric. Fold it in half lengthwise, placing right sides together, and stitch a 1-inch-wide seam along one short edge and the long edge. Clip the corners, turn the box right side out, press the seam allowances to the inside along the opening edges, and whipstitch them together. Pin the flower box to the front wall and hand stitch it in place.

6. Cut each of the yellow felt squares into a flower-blossom shape. We used the classic kindergarten scallop design (**Figure O**), but you can cut them in whatever shape pleases you. Cut a small round center piece from red fabric for each blossom. Glue or tack a center piece to each blossom, and then glue or tack the blossoms to the front wall above the flower box, at varying heights.

7. To make the flower stems and leaves, cut a 2-yard length of green ribbon. Pin it to the front wall between the blossoms and the flower box, making loops and curls. (This is what we call "abstract impressionist greenery.") Glue or tack the greenery in place.

Making the curtains

1. Cut the red-and-white striped fabric in half widthwise so you have two Curtain pieces, each 36 x 49½ inches. Perform the following procedures for each curtain: Fold and press a 1-inch-wide hem to the wrong side of the fabric along each 36-inch-long edge. Stitch one of these hems in place. At the opposite end, again turn the pressed edge to the wrong side of the fabric, allowing a 4-inch hem. Stitch this hem in place, close to the pressed edge.

2. The remaining length of dowel rod will serve as a curtain rod. Slip the rod through the 4-inch-wide hem on both curtains. Inside the playhouse, tie the ends of the rod to the pipe crossbar that is just above the window, using lengths of red ribbon. If you like the "swagged" effect, make loops of green ribbon and tack them to the inside of the wall below the lower corners of the window. Tuck the bottom of each curtain into one of the loops.

Bird Castle

No creaking doors or dungeons, but perhaps a bluejay as court jester and a few swallows jousting in the clouds. This easy-to-clean "castle in the sky" will keep you entertained all summer. Overall dimensions are 14 x 28 x 36 inches.

Figure A

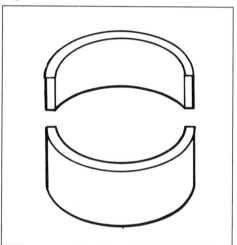

Figure B

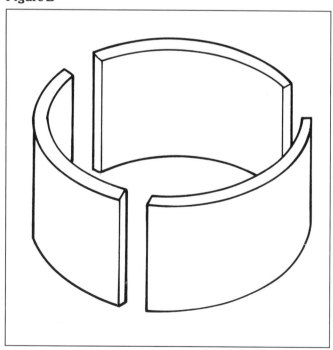

Materials

8 feet of straight 6-inch PVC pipe.
6-inch length of straight 1½-inch PVC pipe.
One 1½-inch PVC end cap.
Thirty-six No. 6 gauge self-tapping sheet metal screws, each ⅝ inch long.
Three ¼-inch bolts, each 2 inches long with two washers and a wing nut.
Finishing nails.
14 x 28½-inch sheet of 3/4-inch exterior grade plywood.
11 feet of ⅜-inch wooden dowel.
6 feet of ¼-inch wooden dowel.
13 linear feet of standard pine 1 x 8.
8 linear feet of ¼ x 1-inch pine lattice.

Cutting the pipe

You will be cutting the pipe and doing some additional drilling, shaping, and beveling on the pipe pieces before you begin the assembly.

1. Cut and label the straight pieces of pipe listed below.

Part	Length	Quantity
A	27¾ inches	1
B	21¾ inches	1
C	16 inches	1
D	3 inches	2
E	1¾ inches	3
F	1¼ inches	1
G	¾ inch	2

2. Pieces **A**, **B**, and **C** will serve as the outer walls of the three towers. To cut the 2-inch-diameter holes for the entryways, measure down from the top of piece **A** and make a pencil mark for the center of each hole at each of the following distances: 4½ inches, 11¼ inches, 18½ inches, and 25¼ inches. On piece **B**, mark the pipe at these distances: 5½ inches, 12¼ inches, and 19 inches. On piece **C**, mark the pipe at: 6½ inches and 13¼ inches.

3. The **E** pieces are cut in half to form the balcony walls. Cut one **E** piece in half as shown in **Figure A**. This will give you two semi-circles. Cut each **E** piece in this manner, so you have six balconies. Label each of the halves **E**.

4. Cut each **G** piece in thirds (**Figure B**). This will give you six balcony-to-pipe connections. Label each of the pieces **G**.

Figure C

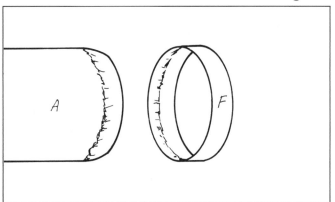

5. Pieces **A** and **F** are beveled so that they will fit snugly together when they are assembled later. Bevel the top of piece **A** on the outside, and one end of piece **F** on the inside (**Figure C**), angling down to a wall thickness of ⅛ inch.

6. Two of the towers will have turrets (**Figure D**). To make the turrets, use the two **D** pieces. Measure around each piece, marking off alternating spaces of 1¼ inches and ¾ inch. The 1¼-inch spaces will be the raised portions. Cut out the ¾-inch spaces, 1¾ inches down from the top.

Cutting the wood

1. A scale drawing of the balcony floor is provided in **Figure E**. Enlarge the drawing and cut six balcony floor pieces from pine. Label each piece **H**.

2. Cut from pine the circular pieces listed below. Label each piece as listed.

Part	Diameter	Quantity
J	6 inches	15
K	6⅝ inches	1
L	6⅛ inches	1
M	5⅝ inches	1
N	5⅛ inches	1
P	4⅛ inches	1
Q	4⅝ inches	1
R	7½ inches	2

3. Cut and label the lengths of ⅜-inch dowel listed below.

Part	Length	Quantity
S	14¼ inches	2
T	27¾ inches	2
U	21 inches	2

4. Cut and label the lengths of ¼-inch dowel listed below.

Part	Length	Quantity
V	2 inches	36

Figure D

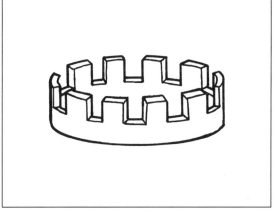

1 square = 1 inch   **Figure E**

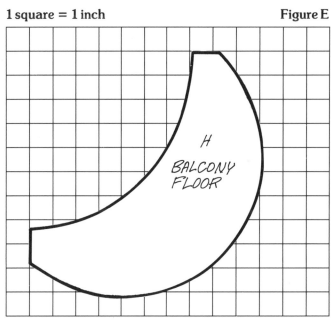

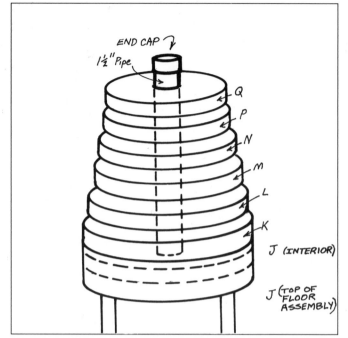

Figure F

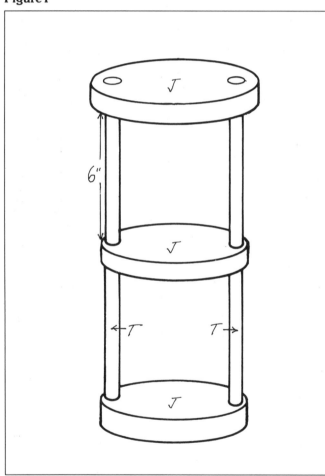

the same, except in height and roof configuration. Each has an inner floor assembly (**Figure F**) that is attached to a roof assembly (**Figures G** and **H**). Balconies are attached to the outer wall of each tower (**Figure I**), and these assemblies are attached to the castle base. The inner floor assembly for each tower slips down inside the outer wall, with the roof fitting snugly on top. The inner assemblies can be removed for cleaning purposes.

Building the floor assemblies

1. Refer to **Figure F** as you build the lift-out floor assemblies. Start with the assembly for the King's Tower, using five **J** pieces and the two **T** pieces. Drill two ⅜-inch-diameter holes through each **J** piece to accomodate the dowels, as shown in **Figure F**. Center each hole ½ inch from the edge, and place them directly opposite each other.

2. Insert a **T** piece into each hole on one **J** piece. Add the remaining **J** pieces, allowing 6 inches between floors. The top and bottom **J** pieces should be flush with the ends of the **T** pieces. Secure the **J** pieces in place with finishing nails.

3. The floor assembly for the Queen's Tower is made in the same manner, using four **J** pieces and the two **U** pieces.

4. Build the floor assembly for the Rook's Tower in the same manner, using three **J** pieces and the two **S** pieces.

Building the roof assemblies

1. Figure G shows the roof assembly for the King's Tower. Drill a hole through the center of each **K**, **L**, **M**, **N**, **P**, and **Q** piece, to match the outer diameter of the 1½-inch straight pipe. Stack these pieces in order of descending size. Insert the 6-inch length of 1½-inch pipe through the aligned holes, and install the end cap on top.

Building the towers

There are three towers, which we have named the King's Tower (the tallest one), The Queen's Tower (middle-sized), and the Rook's Tower (the shortest). Each tower is basically

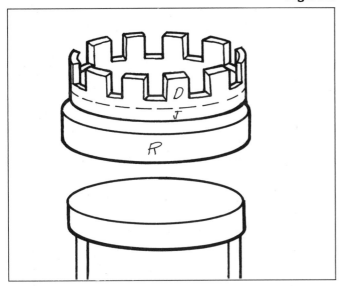

Figure H

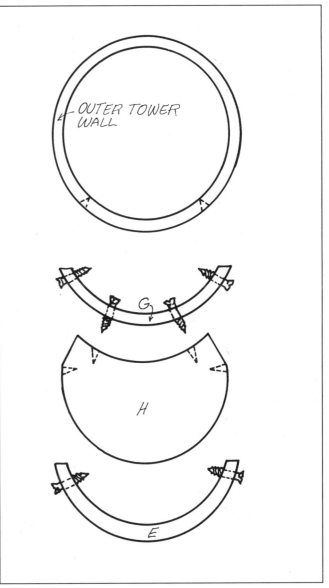

Figure I

2. Center and attach a **J** piece to the bottom of the **K** piece, using glue and finishing nails. Glue the beveled PVC **F** piece, beveled side down, around this **J** piece.

3. Center and glue the assembled roof to the top **J** piece of the tallest floor assembly.

4. To build the roof assembly for the Queen's Tower, refer to **Figure H**. Center and attach a **J** piece to one **R** piece. Glue the turret (**D**) piece around the **J** piece. Glue the assembled roof to the middle-size floor assembly.

5. Repeat the procedures in step 4 to build the roof assembly for the Rook's Tower. Glue this roof assembly to the remaining floor assembly.

Building the balconies

1. Refer to **Figure I** as you assemble the balconies and attach them to the outer tower walls. All pieces are attached using screws. To build one balcony, attach a **G** piece to an **H** piece, as shown, spreading the **G** piece slighty.

2. Attach one of the **E** pieces around the outside edge of the **H** piece, flush at the bottom.

3. Repeat the procedures in steps 1 and 2 to build five additional balconies.

4. Attach one assembled balcony to the outer wall of the King's Tower (piece **A**), 1 inch below the bottom of the uppermost entry hole. To do this, insert screws through the **G** piece, into the tower wall.

5. Repeat the procedures in step 4 to attach the remaining assembled balconies. Place a balcony below each remaining entry hole on the King's Tower outer wall, but do not install a balcony below the bottom entry hole. Place a balcony below each of the two upper entry holes in the Queen's Tower outer wall (piece **B**), and below the top hole only in the Rook's Tower outer wall (piece **C**).

57

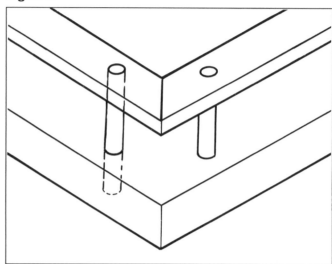

3. Mark the drill points along the center of each rail. On each 28½-inch side, mark the first point ½ inch from the corner, and mark the subsequent points every 2½ inches thereafter. On each 14-inch side, mark the first point ¾ inch from the corner, and mark the subsequent points every 2½ inches thereafter.

4. Drill the holes using a ¼-inch-diameter bit. At each point, drill all the way through the rail and ½ inch into the base. When you have drilled all the holes, remove the holding tacks.

5. Use the **V** pieces as the posts. Insert the posts flush with the top of the trim (**Figure K**) and glue them in place.

Joining the towers and base

1. Drill a ¼-inch-diameter hole through the bottom **J** piece of each floor assembly, at the center point.

2. Assemble the three towers and place them on the base, making sure that no tower is directly over the position where the stand will be attached. Mark the center of each tower on the base, and drill a ¼-inch-diameter hole all the way through the base at each point.

3. Remove the floor assemblies from the tower walls. Slip a washer onto one of the 2-inch bolts and insert the bolt down through the hole in one of the floor assemblies. Slip the floor assembly back into its outer wall. Place the assembled tower on the base, guiding the bolt into the hole in the base. Add another washer, and secure the bolt with a wingnut below the base. Attach each tower in this manner.

4. When you wish to clean the castle, simply remove the wingnuts and lift the inner assemblies free of the outer walls.

Figure J

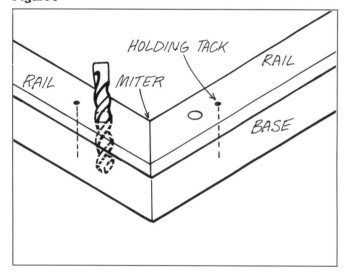

Building the base

The castle base is a plywood rectangle with a railing along each edge. The railing is cut from pine lattice and attached to the base with short lengths of dowel.

1. Cut the rails from pine lattice: two 28½-inch lengths, and two 14-inch lengths. Miter both ends of each piece so they will fit together at the corners, as shown in **Figure J**.

2. The holes that will be drilled to accommodate the dowels must be aligned perfectly between the rails and the plywood base. It will be easier to do this if you temporarily tack the rails to the base, as shown in **Figure J**.

Lawn & Garden Cart

This little number will help you tote an entire array of garden tools, potting soil, and other lawn-care necessities, all at the same time! The wooden barrow is 26 x 40 x 9 inches. The 20-inch wheels allow it to roll smoothly over rough terrain.

Figure A

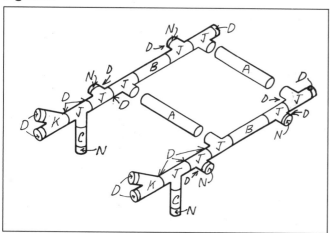

Figure B

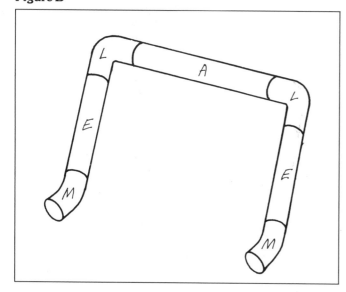

Materials

For the frame:

22 feet of straight 1½-inch PVC pipe.

1½-inch PVC fittings: six 90-degree joints, thirteen T-joints, two Y-joints, six end caps, and two 45-degree joints.

PVC solvent cement, or lots of self-tapping sheet metal screws, each ¾ inch long.

9-inch length of standard pine 2 x 4.

Metal axle rod, ½ inch in diameter and 33½ inches long. You will have to drill a ³⁄₁₆-inch-diameter hole through the diameter of the rod near each end, to house the cotter pins that hold the wheels in place. You can have the drilling done for you, if necessary, at a machine shop.

Two small cotter pins.

Four metal washers, each 1¼ inches in diameter with a ½-inch-diameter center hole.

Two heavy-duty 20-inch bicycle wheels, with tires. We used the type normally found on "dirt" bikes.

For the barrow:

48 x 55-inch piece of ½-inch exterior grade plywood, waferwood, or the equivalent.

Twenty No. 6 gauge flathead wood screws, each 1 inch long.

Four No. 6 gauge flathead wood screws, each 2 inches long.

Wood glue and weatherproofing sealer.

Building the frame

The cart frame consists of four sections: a bottom support section (**Figure A**), a front support section (**Figure B**), a back span section (**Figure C**), and a handle section (**Figure D**). The assembled frame is shown in **Figure E**.

1. The lengths of straight pipe listed below were calculated on the basis of ¾-inch fitting allowances. Check the depth of each fitting and recalculate the lengths, if necessary, to compensate for the difference on each end. (Note: Do not alter the length of the long **G** piece.) Cut and label the pieces of pipe. Label the fittings as listed.

Part	Length	Quantity
A	16½ inches	4
B	12 inches	2
C	9¼ inches	2
D	1⅜ inches	18
E	8¾ inches	4
F	20⅞ inches	2
G	25¾ inches	1
H	17½ inches	1

Fittings:		
J	T-joint	
K	Y-joint	
L	90-degree joint	
M	45-degree joint	
N	End cap	

Figure C

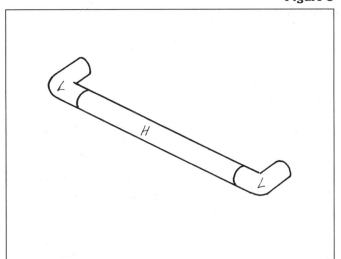

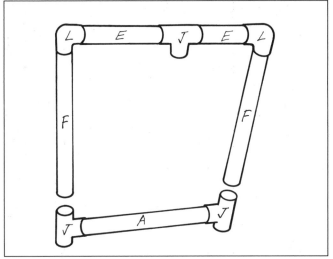

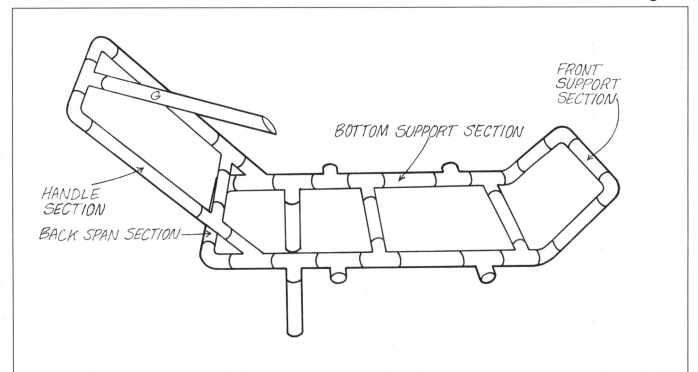

FRONT
SUPPORT
SECTION

BOTTOM SUPPORT SECTION

HANDLE
SECTION

BACK SPAN SECTION

2. The bottom support section is shown in **Figure A**. Begin by assembling separately each long side portion, including the leg (piece **C** with cap **N**) that extends downward. Use a short **D** piece to connect fittings where indicated. Insert the **A** pieces into one of the assembled side portions, and slip the remaining side in place.

3. The front support section is shown in **Figure B**. Assemble the pieces as shown.

4. Assemble the back span section as shown in **Figure C**.

5. The handle section is shown in **Figure D**. Assemble separately the two horizontal portions. Insert the straight **F** pieces into one of these assemblies, and slip the remaining portion in place.

6. The assembled frame is shown in **Figure E**. Join the sections as shown. Cut one end of the **G** piece at a 45-degree angle, and insert the straight end into the open **J** fitting at the top of the handle. You may have to trim this piece to fit when you attach the wooden barrow.

Figure G

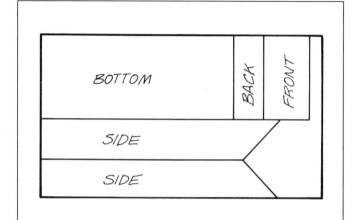

Figure H

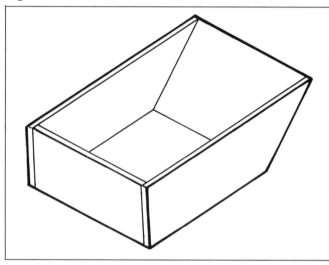

Figure F

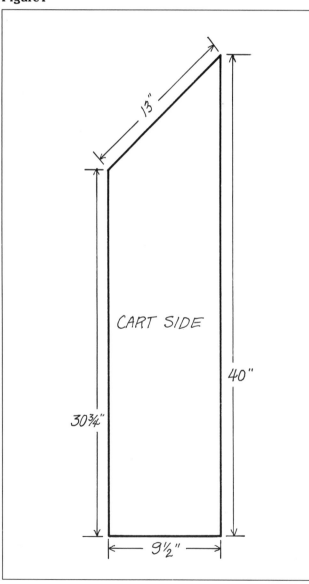

Building the barrow

1. Dimensions for the cart side are provided in **Figure F**. Use the drawing to make a full-size pattern.

2. Cut from plywood the pieces listed below. A cutting diagram is provided in **Figure G**.

       Bottom, 25½ x 30¼ inches – cut one
       Back, 9⅝ x 25½ inches – cut one
       Front, 13⅛ x 25½ inches – cut one
       Side, use pattern – cut two

3. Bevel one long edge of the front piece at a 45-degree angle. This will be the lower edge.

4. The barrow is assembled using simple butt joints secured with glue and 1-inch wood screws. An assembly diagram is provided in **Figure H**. Attach the front, back, and sides so that they cover the edges of the bottom piece. The front and back are sandwiched between the sides, as shown.

5. Coat the barrow thoroughly with sealer.

Figure I

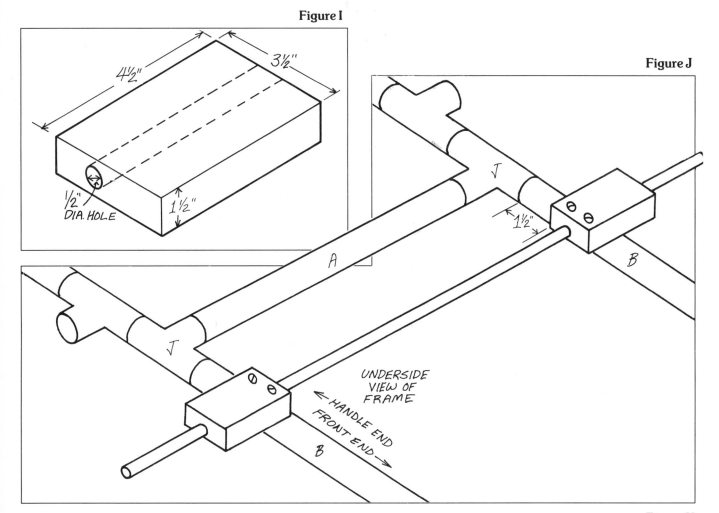

4½"   3½"

½"
DIA. HOLE   1½"

A

1½"

B

J

J

B

UNDERSIDE
VIEW OF
FRAME

← HANDLE END
FRONT END →

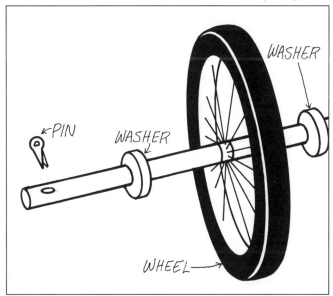

WASHER

PIN   WASHER

WHEEL

Adding the axle and wheels

1. Cut the 9-inch length of pine 2 x 4 in half to form two axle blocks, each 4¼ inches long.

2. Drill a ½-inch-diameter hole straight through the center length of each block, as shown in **Figure I**.

3. Glue the axle blocks underneath the cart frame, one on either side, as shown in **Figure J**. Place each block 1½ inches from the **J** fitting with crossbar **A** that is closest to the back of the frame. Secure each block with two 2-inch wood screws inserted through the block and into the pipe.

4. Insert the axle through the blocks. Glue it in place, leaving equal extensions on each side.

5. The wheel assembly is shown in **Figure K**. At each end of the axle, install a washer, a wheel, and a second washer. Secure the assembly by inserting a cotter pin through the hole and spreading the ends.

Final assembly

Place the wooden barrow on the pipe frame, flush against the front support section. If the long **G** piece that extends forward from the handle section is too long, remove it and trim the flat end a little at a time to avoid overcompensating. Properly trimmed, the angled end of the **G** piece should fit snugly against the back of the barrow. Secure the barrow by inserting 1-inch wood screws down through the bottom, into the frame.

Easy Chair

This easy chair is a companion piece to the sling sofa. It's made in exactly the same way, and is just as soft and comfy. Overall dimensions are 36 x 35 x 35 inches. Once you've built both these pieces, and have the basic idea down pat, build a love seat to match!

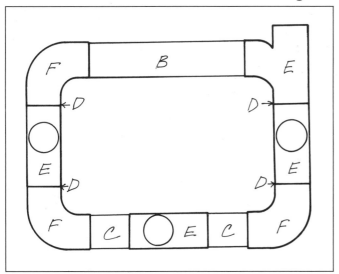

Materials

For the frame:

18 feet of 4-inch straight PVC pipe.

4-inch PVC fittings: eight T-joints and eight 90-degree joints.

PVC solvent cement, or seventy-five No. 6 gauge self-tapping sheet metal screws, each 1 inch long.

For the cover:

4¾ yards of medium- or heavy-weight decorative fabric, at least 45 inches wide.

Thread to match the fabric.

Four 1-inch button forms. (These are button "frames" that you cover with fabric to match whatever you are making.)

Four pieces of quilt batting, each 26 x 40 inches.

Two 20-inch lengths of ¾ x 1-inch slat trim.

Sixteen No. 6 gauge self-tapping sheet metal screws, each 1¼ inches long.

Eight small tacks.

Two 103-inch lengths of nylon webbing, each 2½ inches wide. This is the same material normally used to cover lawn chairs.

Assembling the frame

The frame consists of three sections: two end sections that are mirror images of one another (**Figure A**), and a top span section (**Figure B**). In the final assembly, the end sections are joined by crossbars, and the top span section is added at the back. The assembled frame is shown in **Figure C**.

1. The lengths of straight pipe listed here were calculated on the basis of 1¾-inch fitting allowances. Check the depth of the fittings you purchased and recalculate the lengths of pipe, if necessary, to compensate for the difference on each end. Cut and label the pieces of straight pipe. Label the fittings as listed.

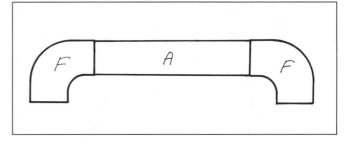

Part	Length	Quantity
A	24½ inches	4
B	23 inches	2
C	8¼ inches	4
D	3½ inches	10

Fittings:

E	T-joint	
F	90-degree joint	

2. One assembled end section is shown in **Figure A**. It's a closed rectangle, consisting mostly of **E** and **F** fittings. Begin by assembling separately each of the vertical portions, using a short **D** piece to connect each two fittings where indicated. Assemble the lower horizontal portion, and insert it into one of the vertical portions as shown. Insert the upper horizontal **B** piece into the same vertical portion, and then install the remaining vertical portion. Be sure the open ends of the fittings are facing the proper direction. It is somewhat tricky to get all the pieces inserted into the fittings as far as they will go, when you're working with pipe this large. You may wish to use a soft mallet to pound the pieces in, and then check to be sure the angles are square by placing the structure against a nice square wall-to-floor corner.

3. Assemble an identical end section, making it a mirror image of the first one by turning the open **E** fittings in the opposite direction.

4. Assemble the top span section as shown in **Figure B**.

Figure C

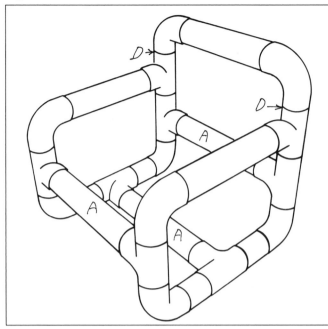

Figure D

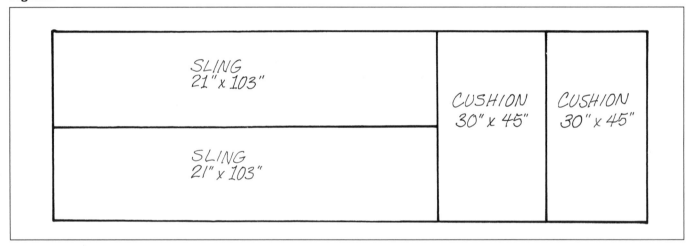

SLING
21" x 103"

SLING
21" x 103"

CUSHION
30" x 45"

CUSHION
30" x 45"

Figure E

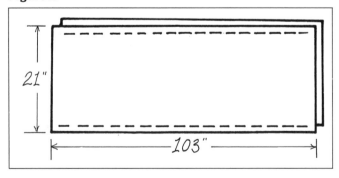

21"

103"

5. The assembled frame is shown in **Figure C**. Use the three remaining **A** pieces to connect the two end sections as shown. Use a short **D** piece at each end to connect the top span section.

Making the cover

The cover consists of two parts: a fabric sling that is attached to the frame by means of wooden slats and screws, and a separate cushion that is attached to the sling by means of upholstery buttons. Cut from decorative fabric the pieces listed below. A cutting diagram is provided in **Figure D**.

    Sling, 21 x 103 inches – cut two
    Cushion, 30 x 45 inches – cut two

Making the sling

1. Place the two Sling pieces right sides together and stitch a ½-inch-wide seam along each long edge. Leave the two short edges open (**Figure E**). Press the seams open. Turn the stitched sling right side out and press it flat, placing the seams at the sides. Topstitch ¼ inch from each seam.

Figure F

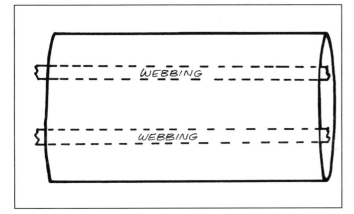

Figure G

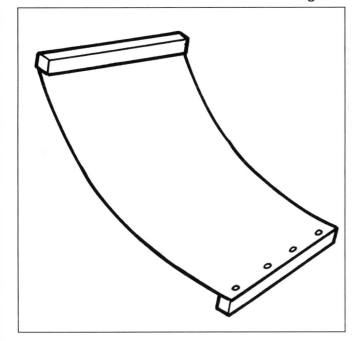

Figure H

Figure I

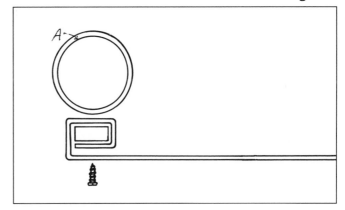

2. Insert the two lengths of nylon webbing between the two sling layers, placing each one 3¾ inches from the center of the sling (**Figure F**). Pin them in place at the ends, making sure that all layers are flat and smooth. Run a line of stitches ½ inch from one short edge of the sling, catching the ends of the webbing in the stitching line. Stitch each webbing strip in place, along both long edges. Finally, run a line of stitches ½ inch from the opposite short edge of the sling. Trim off any webbing material that extends beyond the sling.

3. Place the sling on a flat surface. Place one of the wooden slats underneath the sling, aligned with one short edge (**Figure G**). Secure it with a few small tacks. Attach the remaining slat to the opposite short edge of the sling in the same manner, but place it on top.

4. At the end with the slat on top, roll the slat over and over, one complete turn, keeping the sling fabric smooth and taut. It should look like the end view drawing in **Figure H** when you're finished.

5. Place this end of the sling against the bottom of the top span section on the pipe frame, as shown in the cross-section end view drawing, **Figure I**. Be sure that the sling is placed as shown, with a double thickness of fabric underneath the slat and the remaining length extending out behind the back of the frame. Secure the sling in place by inserting eight 1¼-inch sheet metal screws through the sling and slat, into the pipe. Space the screws evenly along the pipe. To facilitate inserting the screws, pre-drill the holes using a bit that is slightly smaller in diameter than the screw shanks.

67

Figure J

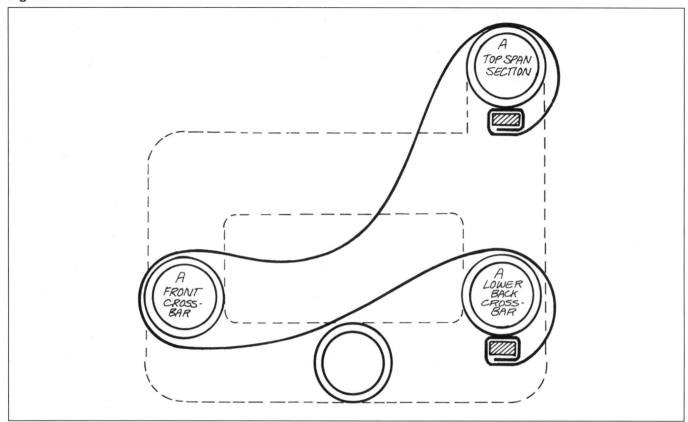

Figure K

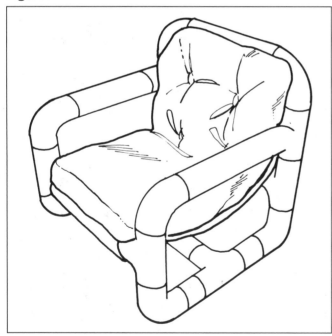

6. Figure J shows the sling properly woven around and through the frame. Wrap it up and over the top span section, then around the outside of the front crossbar from top to bottom. Pull it again toward the back of the frame, over the lower

crossbar at the back. As you hold the end of the sling behind the back of the frame, the slat should be on the bottom. Roll it under, one complete turn, as you did at the opposite end. Place it underneath the lower back crossbar, as shown, and secure it with the eight remaining screws. The sling should sag loosely in the frame.

Making the cushion

1. Pin the two Cushion pieces right sides together and stitch a ½-inch-wide seam along both long edges. Leave both short edges open and unstitched. Press the seams open and turn the stitched cushion right side out. Press the seam allowances to the inside along the short raw edges.

2. Stack the four quilt batting pieces evenly and tack them together in a few spots. Insert the batting inside the cushion and whipstitch the open edges together, folding the corners neatly to accommodate the thickness of the batting.

3. Cover each of the button forms with decorative fabric, following the manufacturer's instructions on the package.

4. To attach the cushion to the sling, first push down on the seat portion of the sling to take up all the slack. The lower portion of the sling, between the front and lower back crossbars, should be taut. Place the cushion on the seat portion of the sling. Use the covered buttons to attach the cushion to the sling, placing them as shown in **Figure K**. To attach each button, stitch back and forth several times, all the way through the cushion and sling. We also tacked the upper edge of the cushion to the sling.

Sling Sofa

Be a Dagwood! If you can't get a quiet nap in the living room, build this comfortable sling sofa for the den. There's 6 feet of stretching room, with a cushioned sling to sink into, and you won't find yourself rolling off the edge! Overall dimensions are 80 x 35 x 35 inches.

Figure B

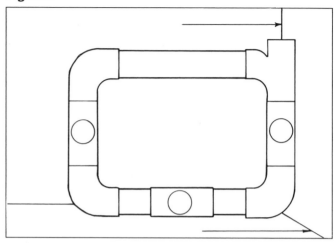

Figure B

Figure A

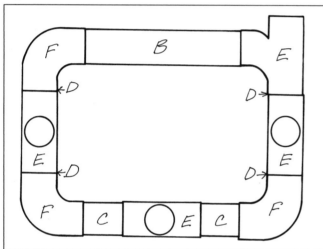

Figure A

Materials

For the frame:

33 feet of 4-inch straight PVC pipe.

4-inch PVC fittings: eight T-joints and eight 90-degree joints.

PVC solvent cement, or seventy-five No. 6 gauge self-tapping sheet metal screws, each 1 inch long.

For the cover:

13½ yards of medium- or heavy-weight decorative fabric, at least 54 inches wide.

Thread to match the fabric.

Four pieces of quilt batting, each 42 x 64 inches.

Two bags of polyester fiberfill.

Ten 1-inch button forms. (These are button "frames" that you cover with fabric to match whatever you're making.)

Two 64-inch lengths of ¾ x 1-inch slat trim.

Forty-four No. 6 gauge self-tapping sheet metal screws, each 1¼ inches long.

A handful of small tacks.

Two 109-inch lengths of nylon webbing, each 2½ inches wide. This is the same material commonly used to cover lawn chairs.

Assembling the frame

The sofa frame consists of two identical end sections (**Figure A**) that are mirror images of one another. Each section forms one end of the sofa. In the final assembly, the two end sections are joined by a top span section (**Figure C**) and long crossbars. The assembled frame is shown in **Figure D**.

1. The lengths of straight pipe listed below were calculated on the basis of 1¾-inch fitting allowances. Check the depth of the fittings and recalculate the lengths, if necessary, to compensate for the difference on each end. Cut and label the pieces of straight pipe. Label the fittings as listed below.

Part	Length	Quantity
A	68½ inches	4
B	23 inches	2
C	8¼ inches	4
D	3½ inches	10

Fittings:

E	T-joint	
F	90-degree joint	

2. One assembled end section is shown in **Figure A**. It's a closed rectangle, consisting mostly of **E** and **F** fittings. Begin by assembling the two vertical portions, using a short **D** piece to connect each two fittings where indicated. Assemble the lower horizontal portion as shown. Be sure that the open ends of all fittings are facing the proper direction. Insert the assembled lower horizontal portion and the top horizontal **B** piece into one of the vertical side portions. Finally, install the remaining vertical side portion. The tricky part, in working with this large pipe, is getting the pipe all the way into the fittings so that everything is truly square. You might want to find a nice square wall-to-floor corner to butt the parts against as you work (**Figure B**).

Figure C

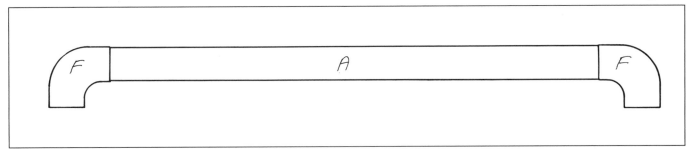

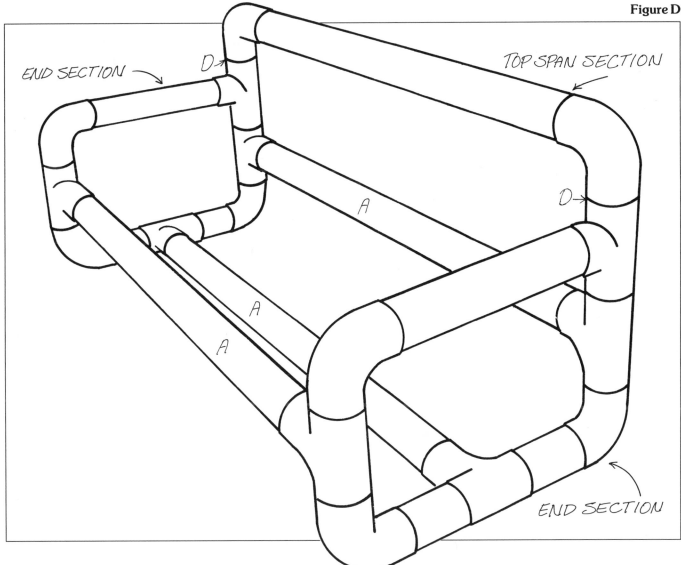

3. Assemble an identical section, making it a mirror image of the first one by turning the open ends of the **E** fittings in the opposite direction.

4. Assemble the top span section as shown in **Figure C**.

5. The assembled frame is shown in **Figure D**. Use the remaining long **A** pieces where indicated to connect the two end assemblies. Use a short **D** piece at each end to attach the top span section.

Making the cover

The cover consists of three separate parts: a fabric sling that is reinforced with webbing straps, a cushion, and pillows. The sling is attached to two wooden strips that are secured to the pipe frame with screws. The cushion is attached to the sling with upholstery buttons. We made two large pillows to match. Cut from decorative fabric the pieces listed below. A cutting diagram is provided in **Figure E**.

Figure E

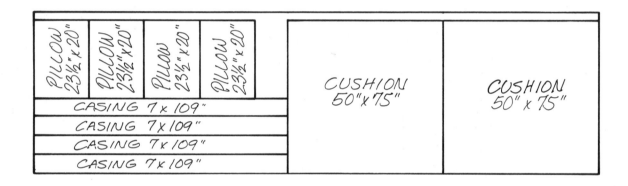

SLING END 5"x109" | SLING END 5"x109"

SLING 49"x109" | SLING 49"x109"

PILLOW 23½"x20" | PILLOW 23½"x20" | PILLOW 23½"x20" | PILLOW 23½"x20"

CASING 7x109"
CASING 7x109"
CASING 7x109"
CASING 7x109"

CUSHION 50"x75" | CUSHION 50"x75"

Figure F

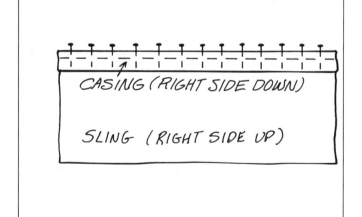

CASING (RIGHT SIDE DOWN)

SLING (RIGHT SIDE UP)

Sling, 49 x 109 inches, cut two
Sling End, 5 x 109 inches, cut two
Sling Casing, 7 x 109 inches, cut four
Cushion, 50 x 75 inches, cut two
Pillow, 20 x 23½ inches, cut four

Making the sling

1. To make the top layer of the sling, place one Sling piece right side up on a flat surface. Place one Casing piece on top, right side down, aligning one long edge of the Casing piece with one long edge of the Sling piece. Pin and then stitch a ½-inch-wide seam along this long edge only (**Figure F**). Press the seam open.

2. Stitch one End piece to the remaining long edge of the Casing piece in the same manner.

3. Stitch a Casing piece to the opposite long edge of the same Sling piece, just as you did the first one. Stitch the remaining End piece to this Casing piece. Press all seams open.

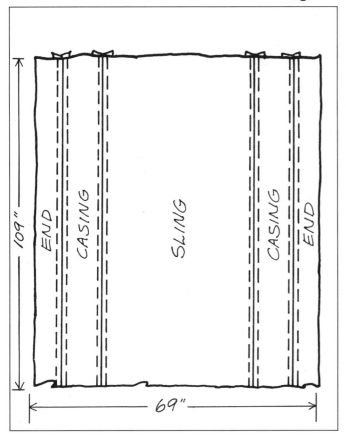

Figure G

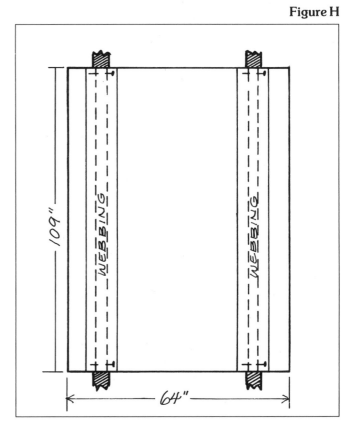

Figure H

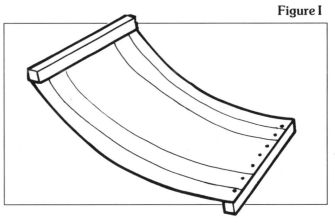

Figure I

4. To strengthen the seams, topstitch through the fabric and the seam allowance, ¼ inch from each seam, on each side (**Figure G**).

5. To make the bottom layer of the sling, stitch each of the remaining Casing pieces to the remaining Sling piece as you did for the top layer. Press the seams open and topstitch.

6. Place the assembled top layer right side up on a flat surface. Place the assembled bottom layer on top, right side down, aligning one long edge of the bottom layer with one long edge of the top layer. Pin and then stitch a ½-inch-wide seam, press the seam open, and topstitch.

7. Reposition the two layers, folding them right sides together, so that the two remaining long edges are aligned. Stitch the seam, press, and topstitch.

8. Turn the assembled sling right side out and place it on a flat surface so that the End pieces are evenly folded at the sides and the top-layer seams are aligned with the bottom-layer seams. Insert a length of nylon webbing between the upper and lower Casing pieces at each side of the sling (**Figure H**), and pin them in place at the ends. Be sure that all layers are flat and smooth, so the webbing matches the sling exactly. Pin the opening edges together along each end of the sling. Run a line of stitches ½ inch from each open edge through the top and bottom layers, catching the ends of the webbing in the stitching lines.

Attaching the sling to the frame

1. Place the assembled sling on a flat surface. Place one of the lengths of slat trim underneath the sling, aligned with one raw edge as shown in **Figure I**. Secure the sling to the trim using a few small tacks. Attach the remaining length of slat trim along the remaining raw edge of the sling, but place it on top instead of underneath. **Figure I** shows both slats attached properly.

Figure J

Figure K

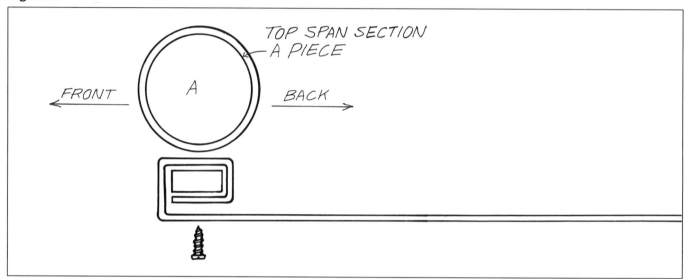

Figure L

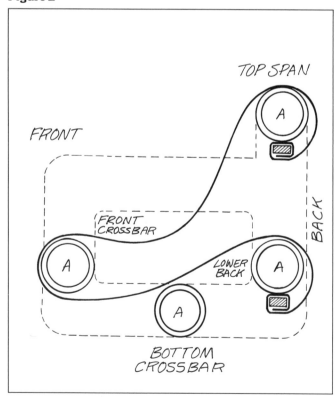

2. At the end with the slat on top, roll the slat over and over, one complete turn, keeping the fabric smooth and taut. **Figure J** shows an end view of what this should look like when you're finished.

3. Place this assembly underneath the top span section of the sofa frame, as shown in the cross-section end view, **Figure K**. Secure it by inserting twenty-two 1¼-inch sheet metal screws through the fabric and slat, up into the pipe, spacing them evenly along the length. Be sure to place the sling as shown, so that the screws pass through a double thickness of the sling along the bottom of the slat, and the remaining portion of the sling hangs behind the frame. To facilitate inserting the screws, pre-drill each hole using a bit slightly smaller than the diameter of the screw shanks.

4. Refer to the cross-section view of the frame in **Figure L** as you weave the sling through the frame to get the proper configuration. Wrap the sling up and over the top span section, and then forward, around the outside of the frontmost **A** piece, from top to bottom. Bring it again to the back of the frame, and wrap it over the lower **A** piece at the back. As you hold the end of the sling out behind this **A** piece, the slat should be on the bottom. Roll the slat under, one complete turn, and place it against the bottom of the lower **A** piece as shown. The sling should not be tight, but should sag loosely in the frame. Secure it to the bottom of the lower **A** piece, using twenty-two evenly spaced screws, as you did at the top.

Making the cushion

1. Pin the two Cushion pieces right sides together and stitch a ½-inch-wide seam along both long edges. Leave both short edges open and unstitched. Turn the cushion cover right side out and press the seam allowances to the inside along the open raw edges.

2. Stack the four pieces of quilt batting evenly, and tack them together in a few spots. Insert the stack of batting inside the stitched cushion cover. Whipstitch the opening edges together at each end, folding them neatly at the corners to accommodate the thickness of the batting.

3. Cover each of the ten button forms with sofa fabric, following the manufacturer's instructions on the package.

4. To attach the cushion to the sling, first press down along the seat portion of the sling, to take up the slack. The portion of the sling that extends from the front crossbar to the lower back crossbar should be taut. Place the cushion on the sling and use the covered buttons to secure it as shown in **Figure M**. Place five buttons, evenly spaced, along a straight line 14 inches from the top of the cushion. Place the remaining five buttons, evenly spaced, along a straight line 14 inches below the first line. To attach each button, stitch several times all the way through the cushion and sling.

Making the pillows

To make each pillow, pin two Pillow pieces right sides together and stitch a ½-inch-wide seam along both long edges and one short edge. Leave the remaining short edge open and unstitched. Turn the pillow cover right side out and press the seam allowances to the inside along the open raw edges. Use one bag of fiberfill to stuff the pillow, and then whipstitch the opening edges together.

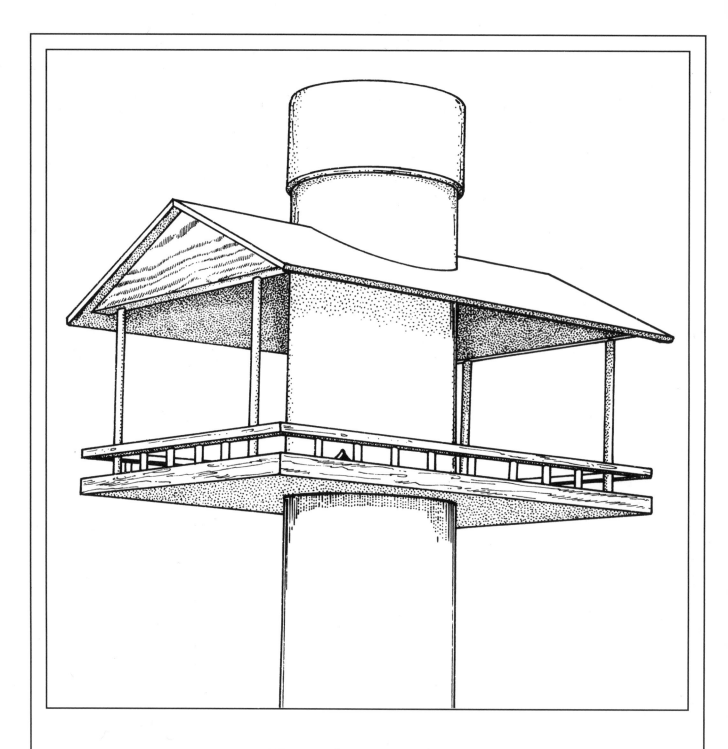

Bird Feeder

What self-respecting bird gourmet could pass up a five-star establishment such as this? It's made of pipe, plywood, pine, and dowels to overall dimensions of 15 x 20 x 15 inches. Don't you wish you could dine out for just a song?

NOTE: ADJUST THE SIZE OF THE CUTOUTS TO THE TYPE OF SEED YOU'RE USING.

Materials

14¼-inch length of straight 6-inch PVC pipe.
One 6-inch PVC end cap.
12⅝ x 18⅝-inch sheet of ¾-inch exterior grade plywood.
16 x 19⅝-inch sheet of ¼-inch exterior grade plywood.
5-foot length of ¼ x ¾-inch slat trim.
4-foot length of ¼-inch wooden dowel.
3-foot length of ⅜-inch wooden dowel.
2 linear feet of standard pine 1 x 4.
Wood filler, carpenter's wood glue, and finishing nails.

Cutting the pipe

The length of pipe serves as a holding chamber for the bird feed. The top is covered with the end cap. To fill it with seed (or other bird yummies), simply remove the cap. The feed is discharged through four cutouts at the bottom of the pipe. Refer to **Figure A** as you make the triangular cutouts.

Assembling the base

The feeder base is a plywood rectangle with a railing assembly attached near each edge. Details of the base assembly are shown in **Figures B** and **C**.

1. The rails are lengths of slat trim. Cut four rails: two 18⅝ inches long, and two 12⅝ inches long. Miter both ends of each rail so they will fit together at the corners (**Figure B**).

2. The ¾-inch plywood piece will serve as the base. The rails are connected to the base with short lengths of dowel. It will be easier to align the dowel holes if you temporarily tack the rails to the base, as shown in **Figure B**.

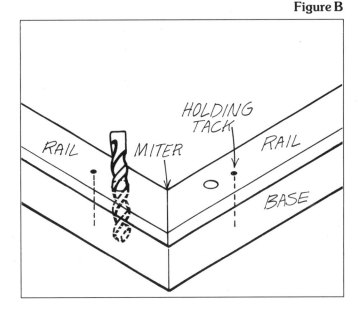

3. Mark the drill points along the center of each rail. On each rail, mark the first drilling point 2 inches from the corner. Mark each subsequent point every 1¾ inches thereafter.

4. Drill a ⅜-inch-diameter hole through the rail and ½ inch into the base at the first and last points on each 12⅝-inch side. Drill a ¼-inch-diameter hole through the rail and ½ inch into the base at each remaining point. Remove the holding tacks and pull the rails loose from the base.

5. Cut the ¼-inch dowel into twenty-six pieces, each 1½ inches long. Cut the ⅜-inch dowel into four pieces, each 7½ inches long.

Figure C

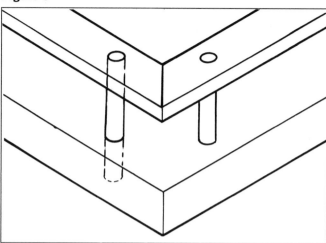

Figure D

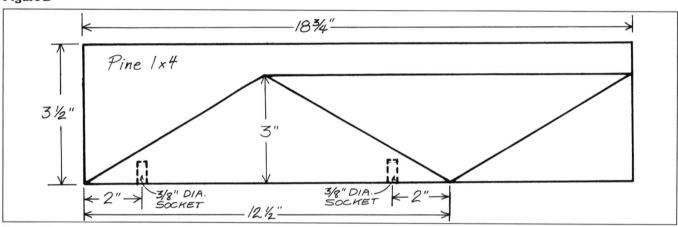

Pine 1x4

18¾"

3½"

3"

2"

3/8" DIA. SOCKET

3/8" DIA. SOCKET

2"

12½"

Figure E

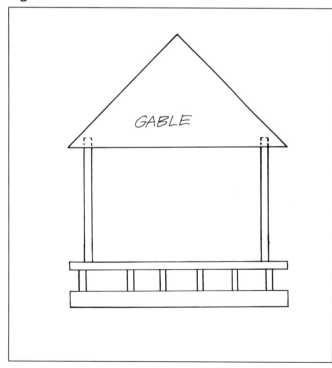

GABLE

6. Glue a length of dowel into each hole in the base. Of course, use the larger dowels for the larger holes, and the smaller dowels for the smaller holes. Spread a little glue around the top of each smaller dowel, and install the rails. The larger dowels will extend up above the rails, but the rails should be flush with the tops of the smaller dowels.

Assembling the roof

1. A cutting diagram for the two gables is provided in **Figure D**. Cut two gables from the pine 1 x 4.

2. The gables are drilled to accommodate the dowels that extend up above the rails on the base. Drill a ⅜-inch-diameter socket up into the longest edge of one gable, placing the center of the socket 2 inches from the end. Drill an additional socket into this gable in the same manner, 2 inches from the opposite end of the same edge. Drill the remaining gable in the same manner.

3. Attach the gables to the base assembly by glueing the dowel ends into the sockets (**Figure E**).

4. The ¼-inch plywood piece is cut in half lengthwise to form the two roof panels. Since one long edge of each panel must be beveled to form the roof peak, you can do both jobs at one time if you set your saw at a 25-degree angle to cut the plywood in half. Turn one of the halves end for end, and

Figure F

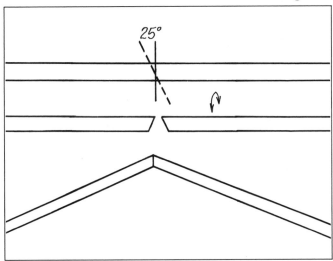

Figure H

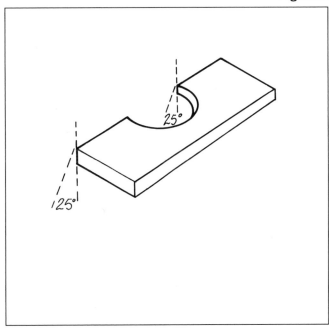

1 square = 1 inch

Figure G

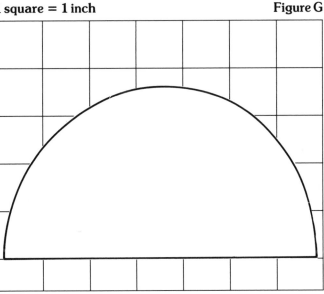

Figure I

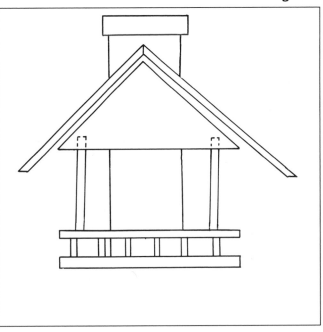

you will have the proper pitch for your roof (**Figure F**). Do not glue the roof panels together just yet.

5. The pipe that serves as the holding chamber is inserted through a hole in the roof. Since the panels will be angled, the hole will not be a perfect circle. A scale drawing for one-half of the hole is provided in **Figure G**. Enlarge it to make a full-size pattern. Use your saw with the blade still set at a 25-degree angle, and cut a half hole into the center of the beveled edge of each roof panel as shown in **Figure H**.

6. Place the holding chamber pipe on the plywood base, and place the roof panels over the gables with the angled edges butted together to form the peak (**Figure I**). When you're sure it's a good fit, glue the roof panels to each other and to the gables. Secure with finishing nails.

7. Fill all gaps in the roof assembly with wood filler, to ensure a water-tight fit.

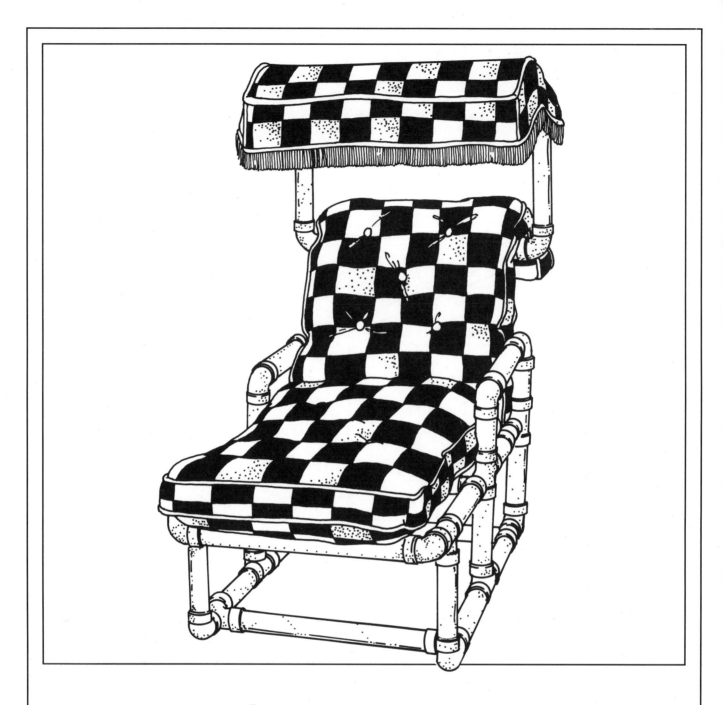

Chaise Lounge

This chaise is perfect for sunbathing in the yard or for a quiet afternoon nap on the shaded patio. It's also a great setting if you want to pose languidly, a`la Bette Davis, while keeping the sun off your face. Overall dimensions are 25 x 46 x 45 inches. You can easily alter the width and length to fit a cushion of a different size.

Materials

For the frame:

50 feet of straight 1½-inch PVC pipe.

1½-inch PVC fittings: four double T-joints, twenty-two T-joints, sixteen 90-degree angle joints, and two 45-degree angle joints.

PVC solvent cement or a multitude of No. 6 gauge self-tapping sheet metal screws, each 1 inch long.

4 x 4-foot sheet of ½-inch exterior grade plywood, waferwood, or the equivalent.

Twelve No. 6 gauge flathead wood screws, each 1 inch long.

Cushion: A standard-size cushion approximately 23 inches wide and 40 to 48 inches long will fit the chaise.

For the canopy cover:

1½ yards of 36-inch-wide waterproof fabric.

5 yards of fringe.

Cutting the pipe

The lengths of pipe listed below were calculated on the basis of ¾-inch fitting allowances. Check the depth of each fitting and, if necessary, recalculate the lengths to compensate for the difference on each end. Cut and label the lengths of straight pipe listed below. Label the fittings as listed.

Part	Length	Quantity
A	16½ inches	4
B	10½ inches	6
C	6½ inches	2
D	5 inches	4
E	14 inches	4
F	10¾ inches	2
G	21 inches	4
H	1⅜ inches	18
J	11½ inches	3
K	6¼ inches	2
L	8½ inches	2
M	11½ inches	2
N	22 inches	2
P	14½ inches	2
Q	4½ inches	2
R	3 inches	2

Fittings:

S	90-degree joint
T	T-joint
U	45-degree joint
V	Double-T joint

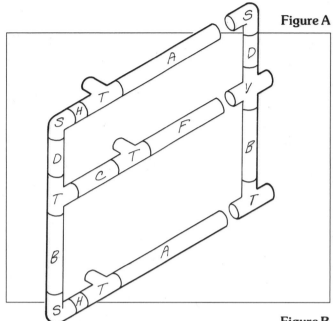

Figure A

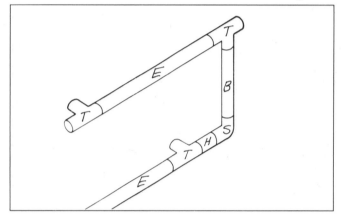

Figure B

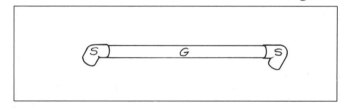

Figure C

Building the frame

The chaise lounge frame consists of seven sections: two identical side sections (**Figure A**), two identical front sections (**Figure B**), a front span section (**Figure C**), a back section (**Figure D**), and a canopy frame (**Figure E**). The side and front sections are joined together in pairs to form the two sides of the frame (**Figure F**). The back section, three crossbars, and the front span section serve to connect the two frame sides (**Figure G**). The canopy frame is attached to the top of the back section (**Figure H**).

Figure E

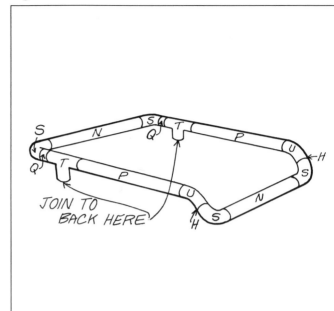

Figure D

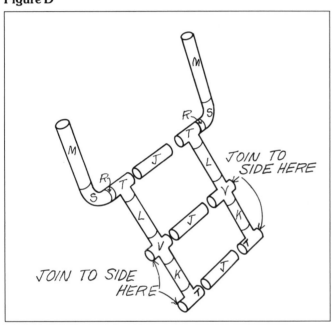

Figure F

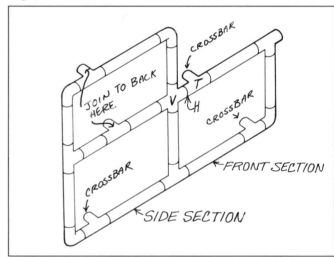

1. One side section is shown in **Figure A**. Assemble the pieces that form the vertical portion on the left side of the drawing, and then assemble and add the horizontal portions. Finally, assemble the vertical portion shown on the right side of the drawing, and slip it in place. Make sure that the open ends of the fittings face the direction shown. The short **H** pieces will not show when the section is assembled properly. They will be covered completely by the fittings they connect.

2. Assemble an identical side section, making it a mirror image of the first one by turning the open ends of the middle **T** fittings in the opposite direction. These **T** fittings should face what will be the center of the chair on each side section.

3. One front section is shown in **Figure B**. This is a very straightforward assembly. Start at one end and join the pieces as shown, working your way around to the other end.

4. Assemble an identical front section, making it a mirror image of the first one by turning the open end of each **T** fitting

in the opposite direction.

5. Assemble the front span section as shown in **Figure C**.

6. The back section is shown in **Figure D**. Assemble each of the identical side portions first, and then join them using the three **J** pieces. Note that **Figure D** is marked to indicate where the back section will be joined to the side sections later in the assembly.

7. The canopy frame is shown in **Figure E**. Assemble the larger portion shown on the left side of the drawing, then assemble the smaller right-hand portion. Join the two assemblies using a short **H** piece on each side. Note that **Figure E** is marked to indicate where the canopy frame will be joined to the back frame section later in the assembly.

8. To begin the final assembly, join one side section to one front section as shown in **Figure F**. Use a short **H** piece to connect the **V** and **T** fittings where indicated.

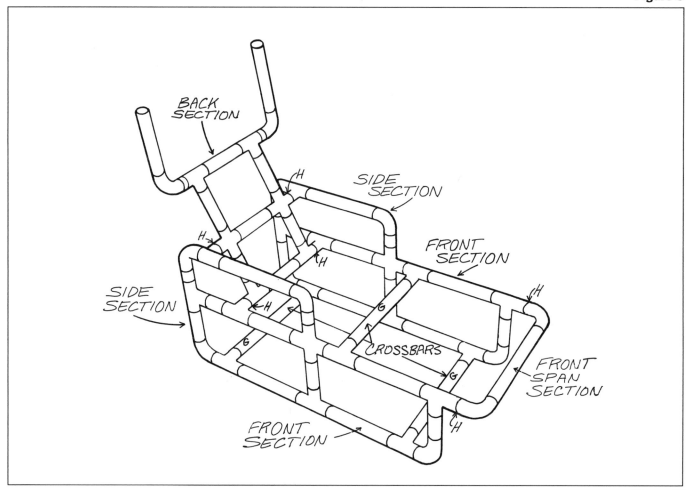

9. Join the remaining side and front sections to form the opposite side of the frame. Note that **Figure F** is marked to indicate placement of the sections and crossbars that will be used to join the two sides in the next step.

10. The assembled frame is shown in **Figure G**. Connect the back section to one assembled frame side where indicated in **Figures D** and **F**, using a short **H** piece to join each pair of fittings. Insert a crossbar (**G** piece) into each fitting on the same frame side, where indicated in **Figure F**. Join one end of the front span section to the same frame side where indicated, using a short **H** piece to connect the fittings. Finally, add the remaining frame side to the open ends of the crossbars and center sections in the same manner.

11. Install the canopy frame on top of the back section. The entire assembled frame is shown in **Figure H**. Secure the canopy frame using screws.

Adding the wooden parts

1. Cut one of each of the following pieces from ½-inch plywood or waferwood:

Seat, 18½ x 41¼ inches
Seat Back, 13½ x 20 inches
Canopy Top, 27 x 31 inches

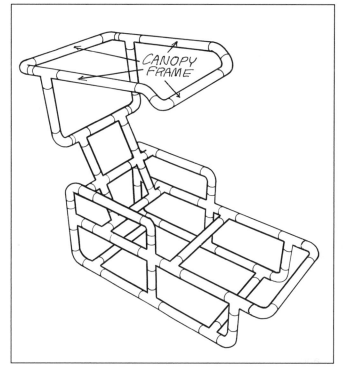

Figure I

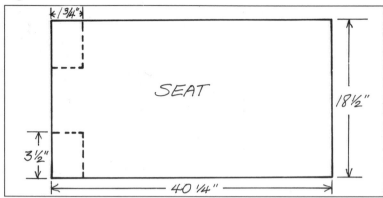

SEAT

1¾"

18½"

3½"

40¼"

Figure J

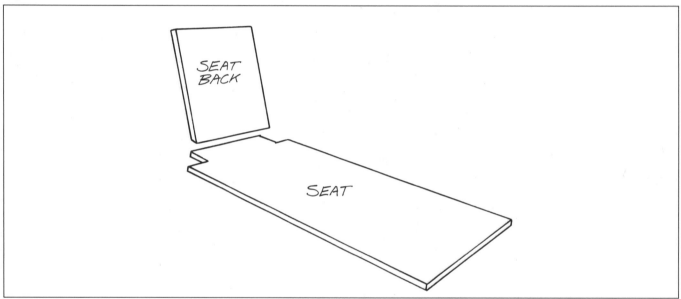

SEAT BACK

SEAT

Figure K

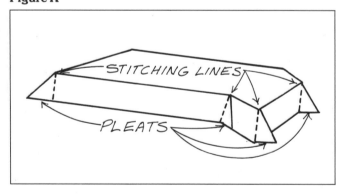

STITCHING LINES

PLEATS

2. Cut a rectangle from each of two adjacent end corners of the Seat piece as shown in **Figure I**. Cut in 1¾ inches from the end and 3½ inches from the side for each cutout.

3. The Seat and Seat Back will fit together as shown in **Figure J**. Attach the Seat to the pipe frame by inserting four wood screws through the Seat and into the frame. Bevel the lower edge of the Seat Back as shown, and attach it to the back section of the frame using four wood screws.

4. Place the Canopy Top on top of the canopy frame, flush with the rear crossbar. It should not extend past the 45-degree fittings near the front of the frame. Attach the Canopy Top using four wood screws.

Making the canopy cover

1. Cut a piece of waterproof fabric 36 x 47 inches.

2. Place the fabric over the Canopy Top with the wrong side of the fabric facing up. Center the fabric so it drapes evenly over all four edges.

3. The canopy cover is pleated as shown in **Figure K**. Pull up and pin a pleat at each of the four corners and at the 45-degree angle points as shown. Remove the cover from the frame and stitch the pleats.

4. Replace the cover on the frame, right side up. Trim off any excess pleat fabric that extends past the bottom edge. Pin the pleats flat against the inside of the bottom edge.

5. Remove the cover from the canopy again, and stitch fringe around the bottom edge.

6. The completed canopy cover can be attached to the wood using short screws, or it can be left unattached.

Patio Canopy Table & Chairs

Break out the playing cards and some tall, cool drinks. There's room for lots of friends around this 4 x 4-foot table, and you don't have to worry about baking in the hot sun! The canopy stands just over 8 feet tall. The chairs are 27 x 23 inches, and 34 inches tall at the back. They will accommodate standard cushions.

Patio Canopy Table

Figure A

Figure A

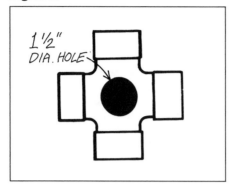

Figure B

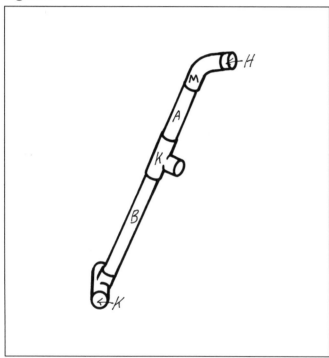

Materials

For the frame:

55 feet of straight 1½-inch PVC pipe.

1½-inch PVC fittings: four double-T joints, eight T-joints, eight 90-degree joints, and sixteen 45-degree joints.

PVC solvent cement or a multitude of No. 6 gauge self-tapping sheet metal screws, each ¾ inch long.

Note: You may wish to purchase an adjustable patio umbrella to use with the table, instead of making the canopy frame and cover shown here. If so, you will need only 26 feet of straight pipe, two double-T joints, no T-joints, and no 45-degree joints. You will still need the eight 90-degree joints.

86

For the canopy cover:

4½ yards of 54-inch-wide canvas or vinyl.

5½ yards of fringe, approximately 1 inch long.

60-inch length of heavy string or nylon cord.

Heavy-duty thread to match the fabric.

Note: If you purchase a patio umbrella, you will not need any of the materials specified for the canopy cover.

For the tabletop:

4 x 4-foot sheet of ¾-inch exterior grade plywood, waferwood, or the equivalent.

Wood sealer.

Eight No. 6 gauge flathead wood screws, 1¼ inches long.

Cutting the pipe

The lengths of straight pipe listed below were calculated on the basis of ¾-inch fitting allowances. Check the depth of each fitting and, if necessary, recalculate the lengths of pipe to compensate for the difference on each end. Cut and label the lengths of pipe. Label the fittings as listed below. (Note: If you purchased a patio umbrella, the list will be revised as follows: no A, B, D, E, or H pieces are required. There will be no T-joints or 45-degree joints to label.)

Part	Length	Quantity
A	13½ inches	4
B	15 inches	4
C	11⅜ inches	4
D	29¼ inches	4
E	98 inches	1
F	20 inches	8
G	22 inches	4
H	1⅜ inches	16
Fittings:		
J	Double-T joint	
K	T-joint	
L	90-degree joint	
M	45-degree joint	

Building the canopy frame

Note: Skip this section if you purchased a patio umbrella.

The canopy frame consists of four identical arm sections (**Figure B**) that are joined together to form the basic frame (**Figure C**). There is an additional center support section (**Figure D**) that adds stability to the long center pole, and four identical span sections (**Figure E**) that connect the lower arms of the basic frame in the final assembly (**Figure F**).

1. A double-T fitting (**J**) serves to connect the four arm sections of the canopy frame. It must be drilled to accommodate the center pole. Cut a 1½-inch-diameter hole into the center of one **J** fitting as shown in **Figure A**. Cut through one side of the fitting only – do not cut a hole in the opposite side of the fitting.

2. Assemble one arm section as shown in **Figure B**. Be sure that the fittings are turned as shown.

Figure C

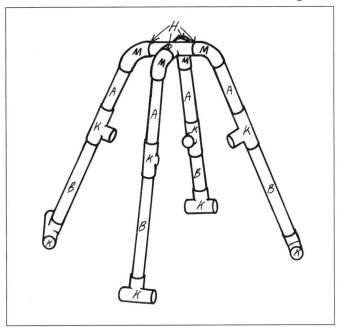

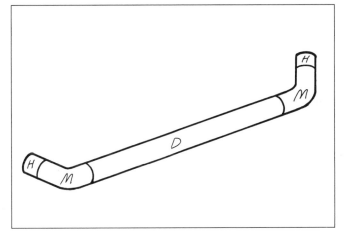

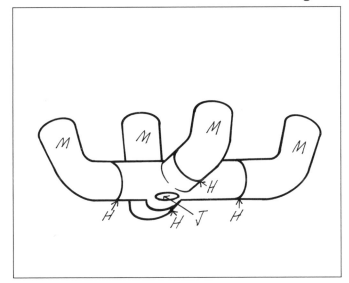

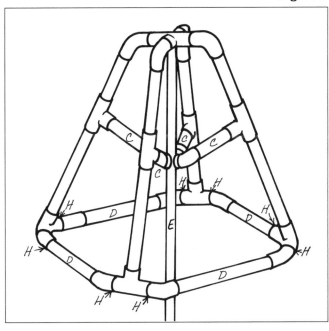

3. Assemble three additional arm sections.

4. Use the **J** fitting with the hole in it to connect the four arm sections as shown in **Figure C**. Be sure that the hole in the fitting is facing downward.

5. The center support section also includes a **J** fitting that must be cut. Cut the same size hole, but this time cut through both sides of the fitting so there is a hole all the way through.

6. Assemble the center support section as shown in **Figure D**, using a short **H** piece to connect each **M** fitting to an open end of the **J** fitting.

7. The span section is shown in **Figure E**. Assemble four span sections as shown.

8. The assembled canopy frame is shown in **Figure F**. First, use four **C** pieces to connect the center support section to the four arm sections. Join the lower ends of the arm sections using the four span sections. Finally, insert the center post (**E**) through the center support section and up into the top fitting.

87

Figure G

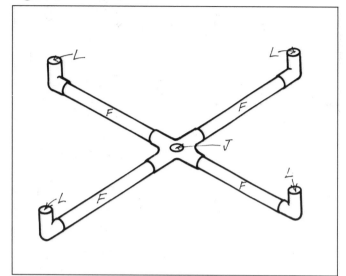

Figure H

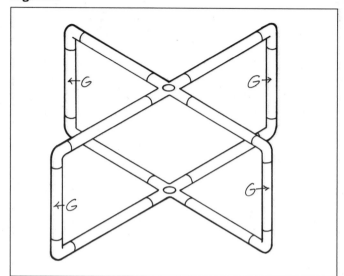

Figure I

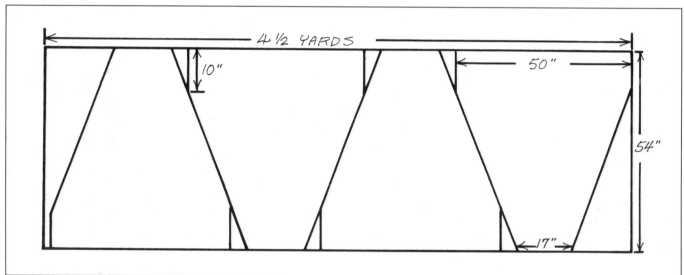

Building the table frame

The table frame consists of two x-shaped sections (**Figure G**). One forms the top of the table frame, and one forms the bottom. In the final assembly, the two sections are connected by four crossbars (**Figure H**).

1. The top section requires a **J** fitting with holes cut in both sides. Cut this fitting as you did the one for the center support section of the canopy frame.

2. Assemble the top section as shown in **Figure G**. Be sure that all of the **L** fittings are facing the direction shown.

3. The bottom section requires a **J** fitting with a hole cut in one side only. Cut this fitting as you did the one for the top of the canopy frame.

4. Assemble the bottom section as you did the top section (**Figure G**). The open ends of the **L** fittings should face the same direction as the hole in the **J** fitting.

5. The assembled table frame is shown in **Figure H**. Place

the bottom section flat on the ground with the open fitting ends and the center hole facing upward. Insert a **G** piece into each of the open **L** fittings. Install the top section, guiding the ends of the **G** pieces into the fittings.

Making the canopy cover

Note: Skip this section if you purchased a patio umbrella.

1. A cutting diagram for the four pieces required to make the canopy cover is provided in **Figure I**. Place your fabric on a flat surface, wrong side up, and plot the corner points of each piece directly on the fabric. Cut the pieces.

2. The stitched cover is shown, wrong side out, in **Figure J**. Pin the four pieces together as shown, placing right sides together. Slip the pinned cover down over the canopy frame, with the wrong side facing up. Adjust the pins so that each seam will run straight down the center of an arm section of the frame.

3. Cut the string or cord into four 15-inch lengths. Pin one length of cord at each corner as shown in **Figure J**.

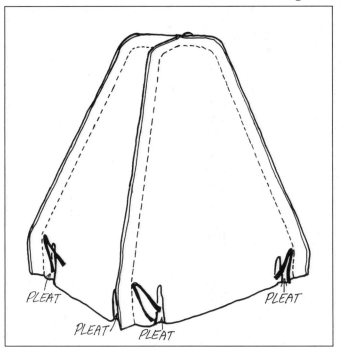

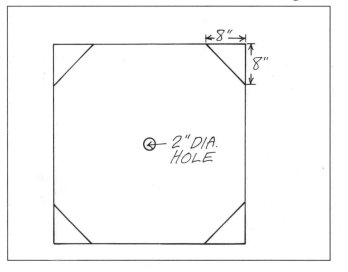

4. Remove the cover from the frame and stitch each seam. Stitch the seams again, close to the first stitching, for extra strength. Stitch the cord to the cover at each corner, over the existing seam line.

5. Trim each seam allowance to 1 inch wide. Turn the cover right side out and replace it on the canopy frame. Tie the cord to the frame at each corner.

6. The canopy cover will not hang perfectly straight around the lower edge because of the curve of the frame. To correct this, pin a pleat approximately 6 inches from each seam at both ends of each side, as shown in **Figure J**. Remove the cover again and stitch the pleats (**Figure K**). Fold each pleat flat against the cover and stitch across the bottom as shown. Trim off any pleat fabric that extends down past the lower edge of the cover.

7. Pin the fringe around the lower edge of the cover and stitch. Replace the cover on the frame and tie it in place.

Making the tabletop

1. Cut the four corners off the 4 x 4-foot plywood piece as shown in **Figure L**. Drill a 2-inch-diameter hole straight down through the center of the plywood.

2. Place the plywood over the table frame, aligning the center holes. To attach the top, insert wood screws through the plywood into the frame, using two screws at each corner.

Final assembly

It's much easier to assemble the two sections if you do it sideways. Lay the table on it's side and insert the center pole through the hole in the table and into the hole in the bottom section of the table frame. Have someone help you lift the assembled canopy table into an upright position, unless you're feeling like Superman today.

Patio Chair

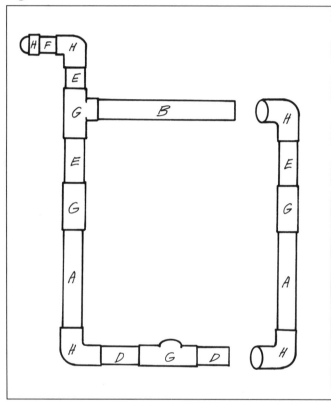

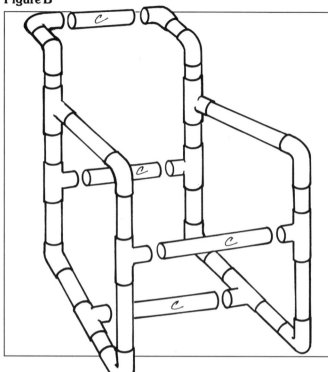

Cutting the pipe

Cut and label the lengths of straight pipe listed below. The fitting allowance used to calculate the lengths was ¾ inch. Check the depth of each fitting and recalculate, if necessary, to compensate for the difference on each end. Label the fittings as listed.

Part	Length	Quantity
A	11 inches	4
B	17¼ inches	2
C	21 inches	4
D	7¼ inches	4
E	5¼ inches	6
F	1⅜ inches	2

Fittings:

G	T-joint
H	90-degree joint

Assembling the frame

The chair consists of two identical side sections (**Figure A**) that are mirror images of each other. In the final assembly, the two sections are joined by four crossbars (**Figure B**).

1. Assemble one side section (**Figure A**). Begin with the longer vertical portion and the two horizontal portions, then assemble the shorter vertical portion and slip it in place.

2. Assemble another side section, identical to the first, but turn the open ends of the **G** fittings in the opposite direction. (All open fitting ends should face what will be the center of the chair.)

3. Use the four **C** pieces to join the two side sections as shown in **Figure B**.

Materials

20 feet of straight 1½-inch PVC pipe.
1½-inch fittings: eight T-joints, and ten 90-degree joints.
PVC solvent cement or 90 self-tapping sheet metal screws.
2 x 4-foot piece of ½-inch-thick exterior plywood, waferwood, or the equivalent.
Six molly bolts, each long enough to accommodate a "wall" ⅝ inch thick.
Four No. 6 gauge flathead wood screws, each 1 inch long.
Cushion: A cushion approximately 22 x 42 x 3 inches, that bends in the middle, will fit this chair. You may prefer to use separate cushions for the seat and back. If you find a bargain in cushions of slightly different size, the chair can easily be altered to fit.
Carpenter's wood glue, and sandpaper.

Figure C

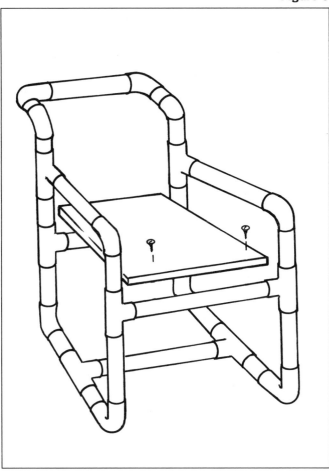

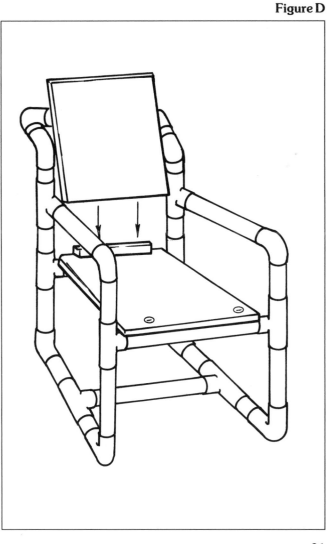

Adding the seat

1. The Seat and Seat Back are cut from plywood. Cut the Seat 19 x 21½ inches, and the Seat Back 19 x 17 inches. In addition, cut a Support Strip 1 x 19 inches.

2. Put the Seat in place (**Figure C**) and attach it to the front crossbar of the chair frame using two of the molly bolts. Attach it to the rear crossbar in the same manner.

3. The Seat Back and Support Strip are placed as shown in **Figure D**. Bevel the lower edge of the Seat Back and the front edge of the Support Strip as shown, so that the Seat Back will tilt slightly toward the rear at a comfortable sitting angle. Glue the Support Strip to the Seat, flush with the rear edge. Insert two of the wood screws through the Support Strip, into the Seat.

4. Attach the Seat Back to the upper crossbar using the two remaining molly bolts, and to the Support Strip using the two remaining wood screws.

Bookcase

Here's a terrific item for any room in the house! With three open shelves and one enclosed case, it will hold scores of books and knickknacks. You might like to make more than one case, or simply build four shelves. Overall dimensions are 37 x 13 x 56 inches.

Materials

For the frame:

30 feet of straight 1½-inch PVC pipe.

1½-inch PVC fittings: four 90-degree angle joints, twenty-four T-joints, and four end caps.

24 feet of straight ¾-inch CPVC pipe.

PVC solvent cement, or lots of No. 6 gauge self-tapping sheet metal screws, each ¾ inch long.

For the case and shelves:

48 x 64-inch piece of ¾-inch veneer-core plywood. Choose a plywood with a nice finish on both sides.

7 x 34-inch piece of ¾-inch walnut or other hardwood that contrasts nicely with the plywood.

4-inch length of ¼-inch wooden dowel rod.

Two spherical wooden drawer pulls, each 1¼ inches in diameter. These normally come with attaching screws but if the ones you purchase do not, you'll need two No. 6 gauge flathead wood screws, each 1½ inches long.

A handful of 4d finishing nails.

Carpenter's wood glue, sandpaper, stain, regular wood filler, walnut wood filler, and a small quantity of wax-type lubricant such as beeswax or hard soap.

Building the frame

The frame consists of two end sections (**Figure A**) that are drilled to accommodate the ¾-inch shelf supports. In the final assembly, the two end sections are joined by shelf supports and crossbars (**Figure E**).

1. The lengths of 1½-inch straight pipe listed below were calculated on the basis of ¾-inch fitting allowances. Check the depth of each fitting and recalculate the lengths, if necessary, to compensate for the difference on each end. Cut and label the lengths of straight pipe. Label the fittings as listed.

Part	Length	Quantity
A	8⅛ inches	2
B	7⅛ inches	16
C	3 inches	2
D	11¼ inches	6
E	1⅜ inches	12
F	31⅜ inches	4

Fittings:

G	End cap	
H	T-joint	
J	90-degree joint	

2. Cut the lengths of ¾-inch straight pipe listed below. There's no need to recalculate for fitting allowances.

Part	Length	Quantity
K	35¾ inches	8

3. One assembled end section is shown in **Figure A**. Begin by assembling the pieces and fittings that form the vertical portion on the left side of the drawing. An exploded view of

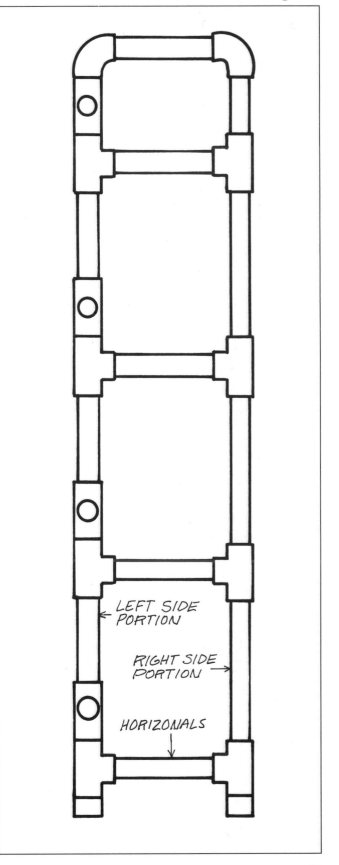

LEFT SIDE PORTION

RIGHT SIDE PORTION

HORIZONALS

Figure C

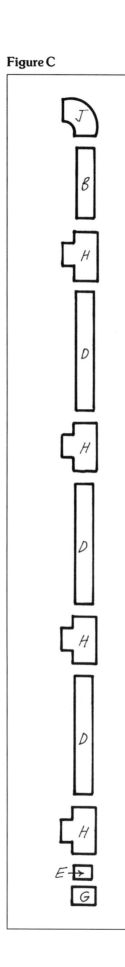

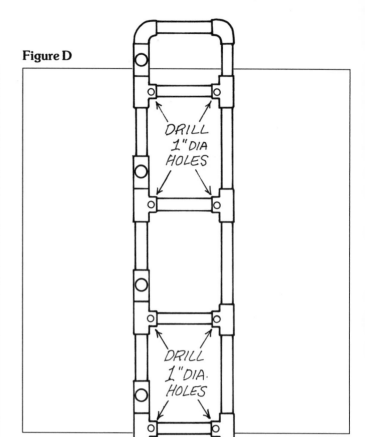

DRILL 1" DIA HOLES

DRILL 1" DIA. HOLES

this portion is provided in **Figure B**. Just assemble the parts as shown, using a short **E** piece to connect fittings where indicated. The **E** pieces will not show when the fittings are inserted as far as they will go. Be sure that the open ends of the fittings are turned in the directions shown.

4. The pieces and fittings that form the vertical portion on the right side are shown in **Figure C**. Assemble this portion as shown.

5. Add the horizontal pieces to the vertical portion that you assembled in step 4. Insert an **A** piece into the top **J** fitting, and a **B** piece into each of the lower **H** fittings as shown in **Figure A**.

6. Install the left vertical portion, as shown in **Figure A**.

7. Repeat the procedures in steps 3 through 6 to build an identical end section. To make it a mirror image of the first one, turn the remaining open **H** fittings so that they face the opposite direction.

8. The two end sections must be drilled to accommodate the ¾-inch shelf supports. Place one end section on a flat surface, with the open ends of the **H** fittings facing up. Drill a 1-inch-diameter hole into the section at each location indicated in **Figure D**. At each location, drill through one side of the fitting-and-pipe connection only. Do not continue to drill out the other side.

9. Drill the remaining end section in the same manner, being sure to align the holes carefully between the sections.

10. The assembled frame is shown in **Figure E**. Prop one end section against a wall, or recruit an assistant to help hold it in an upright position. Insert the shelf supports (**K** pieces) and crossbars (**F** pieces) as shown. Install the remaining end section, and make sure that both end sections are pushed in toward the center as far as they will go.

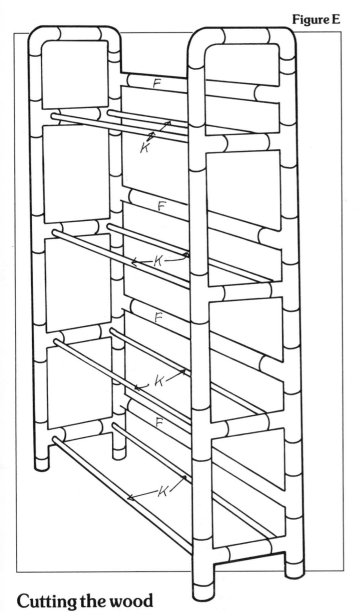

Figure E

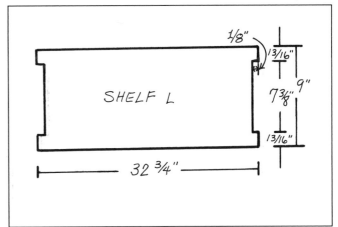

Figure F

SHELF L

1/8"

13/16"

9"

7 3/8"

13/16"

32 3/4"

Figure G

SHELF TRIM

Cutting the wood

Our bookcase has three shelves and an enclosed case. Each is made of plywood, with walnut trim. Cut and label the pieces listed below.

Part	Dimensions	Quantity
Cut from plywood:		
L	9 x 32¾ inches	3
M	7¾ x 31 inches	2
N	8½ x 12¾ inches	2
P	12¾ x 31 inches	1
Q	7¾ x 31½ inches	1
R	6⅞ x 30⅞ inches	1
Cut from walnut:		
S	⅞ x 32½ inches	3
T	¾ x 32½ inches	1
U	¾ x 12¾ inches	2
V	¾ x 30⅞ inches	1
W	¾ x 31 inches	1

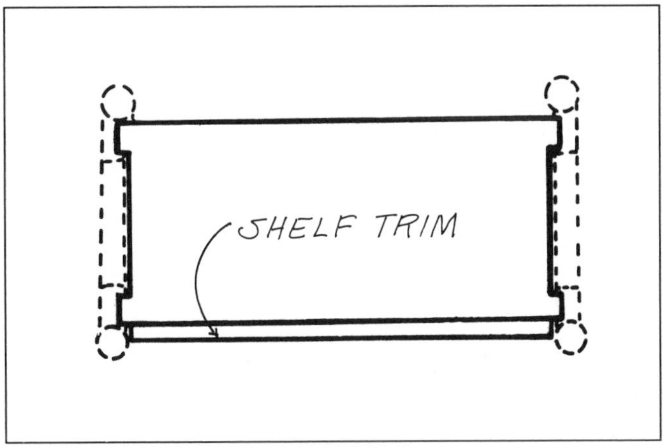

Building the shelves

1. The **L** pieces will serve as the three open shelves. Each must be contoured slightly to fit into the pipe frame snugly. A cutting diagram is provided in **Figure F**. Make a ⅛-inch-wide cutout in both short ends of each **L** piece, as shown.

2. The **S** pieces will serve as the front trim on the three open shelves. Glue an **S** piece to one long edge of each **L** piece, centered between the ends (**Figure G**). Secure the assembly with finishing nails, recess the nails, and cover the holes with walnut wood filler.

3. Sand and stain the shelves.

4. Place one of the shelves on two aligned shelf supports, on the pipe frame. Insert the remaining two shelves as you did the first one. You can place them on any three levels. (The remaining open level will house the enclosed case.) We left the shelves unattached, as there's very little chance that they will fall off. You can attach them if you wish, by inserting 1-inch wood screws through the shelves into the supports.

Figure I

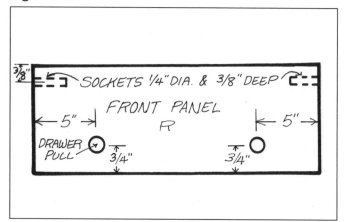

SOCKETS ¼" DIA. & ⅜" DEEP

FRONT PANEL
R

5"

5"

DRAWER PULL

¾"

¾"

3/8"

Figure H

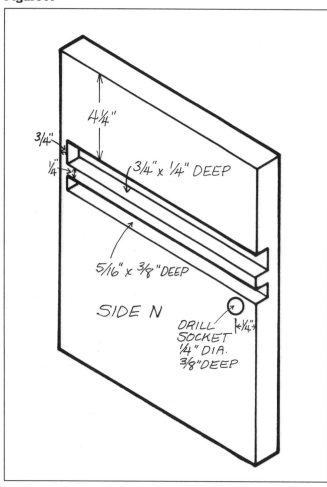

4¼"

¾"

¼"

¾" x ¼" DEEP

5/16" x ⅜" DEEP

SIDE N

DRILL SOCKET ¼" DIA. ⅜"DEEP

¼"

Building the case

The remaining wooden pieces are assembled to make the enclosed case. It is a rectangular plywood box with one shelf, that is assembled using butt joints for the most part. A front panel covers the lower portion of the case, below the shelf. It can be raised and slid back into the case by means of dowel pegs that slide along grooves cut into the side case pieces.

1. The two **N** pieces will serve as the sides of the case. You will need to cut two dadoes in each **N** piece: one to accommodate the shelf, and one to accommodate the dowel peg that allows the front panel to move. You'll also need to drill a socket into each piece, to accommodate a dowel peg that will keep the panel from falling down when it's supposed to stay up. **Figure H** shows placement of the dadoes and sockets. First, cut a ¾-inch-wide dado, ¼ inch deep, starting at one long edge of the piece and ending ¾ inch from the opposite long edge. Place this dado 4¼ inches from the top short edge, as shown. Cut the second dado 5/16 inch wide and ⅜ inch deep, starting and ending at the same positions. Allow a ¼-inch space between the dadoes. Drill a ¼-inch-diameter socket, ⅜ inch deep, just below the second dado. Place the center of the socket ¼ inch from the front long edge.

2. Cut two dadoes and drill a socket into the remaining **N** piece in the same manner, but on the opposite surface. The two **N** pieces should be mirror images of each other.

3. The **R** piece will serve as the front panel. Drill a ¼-inch-diameter socket, ⅜ inch deep, into both short edges of the **R** piece (**Figure I**). Place the center of each socket ⅜ inch from the top long edge, as shown. Attach the two drawer pulls, placing them ¾ inch from the bottom long edge and 5 inches from the respective sides. Sand the front and back of the upper edge vigorously to round off the corners.

4. Cut the dowel rod into four ¾-inch lengths. Glue one length into each of the sockets in the front panel. Glue another length into the socket you drilled in one side piece (**R**) in step 1. Glue the remaining length into the socket in the other side piece. Tap the dowels with a hammer to make sure they are inserted into the sockets as far as they will go.

Practice Projects

Trivet, page 13

Garden Seat, page 14

Wine Rack, page 15

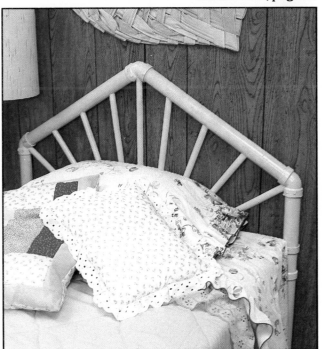

Headboard/Trellis, page 17

Serving Cart, page 130

Glider, page 21

Cat House, page 150

Coffee Table, page 140

Etagere, page 43

Bird Feeder, page 76

End Table, page 159

Easy Chair, page 64

Sling Sofa, page 69

Bar Stool, page 143

Figure J

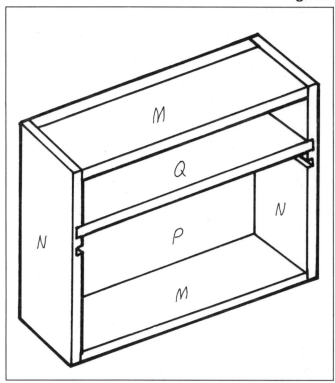

Figure K

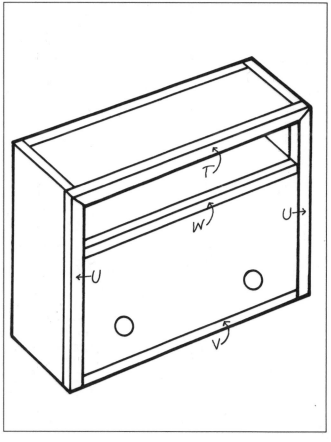

5. The **V** piece will serve as trim along the bottom of the front panel. Glue the **V** piece to the lower edge and secure it with finishing nails. Recess the nails and cover the holes with walnut wood filler.

6. The basic case is assembled as shown in **Figure J**. Glue the top (**M**), bottom (**M**), back (**P**), and shelf (**Q**) between the two sides, butting the edges as shown and inserting the ends of the shelf into the wider dadoes in the side pieces. The top, bottom, shelf, and sides should be flush at the front. Secure the joints with recessed finishing nails, and cover the holes with regular wood filler.

7. The **W** piece will serve as trim on the shelf. Glue the trim to the front edge of the shelf. Secure it with recessed finishing nails and cover the holes with walnut filler.

8. The **T** and **U** pieces will serve as trim on the top and side pieces. Miter both ends of the **T** piece and one end only of each **U** piece, using a 45-degree angle for each miter so the pieces will fit together at the upper corners (**Figure K**). Slide the front panel in place, inserting the dowels that extend from the edges into the narrow dadoes in the case sides. Glue the top and side trim pieces in place, secure them with recessed finishing nails, and cover the holes with walnut filler.

9. Sand and stain the case.

10. Lift the front panel and lubricate the narrow dadoes with beeswax or hard soap. Test the action of the panel to make sure it will slide easily in and out.

11. Slide the assembled case into the remaining open level of the pipe frame. You can leave it unattached, or secure it with wood screws as you did the shelves.

Patio & Game Room Bar

Hitch up to the bar, folks! This easy-to-build project has a pipe frame and a plywood body with lots of storage space. It can even be used as a workbench. Overall dimensions are 40 x 61 x 32 inches, and you can upholster the top with vinyl or leather for a richer look.

Materials

50 feet of straight 1½-inch PVC pipe.

1½-inch PVC fittings: six 90-degree angle joints, twenty-five T-joints, and seven end caps.

PVC solvent cement or a double handful of No. 6 gauge self-tapping sheet metal screws, each 1 inch long.

Two sheets of ¾-inch interior grade plywood. We used baltic birch because it has a nice finish.

Two 8-foot lengths of ¼ x 2-inch slat trim.

Carpenter's wood glue, 3d finishing nails, and molly bolts or wood screws to attach the plywood to the pipe frame.

Cutting the pipe

The required lengths of pipe listed below were calculated on the basis of ¾-inch fitting allowances. Check the depth of each fitting and, if necessary, recalculate the lengths of pipe to compensate for the difference on each end. Cut and label the straight pieces of pipe. Label the fittings as listed.

Part	Length	Quantity
A	1⅜ inches	10
B	4½ inches	2
C	5 inches	3
D	6 inches	4
E	9 inches	4
F	11½ inches	8
G	14¼ inches	2
H	16¼ inches	6
J	26⅜ inches	2
K	25 inches	4
L	24½ inches	2
Fittings:		
M	T-joint	
N	End cap	
P	90-degree joint	

Cutting the wood

Cutting dimensions for the trim and plywood pieces required for the counter top and the bar box are listed below. Our bar has only one shelf and one divider, but you may want more. For each additional shelf, cut one Shelf piece and two Shelf Supports. Cutting diagrams for the larger pieces are provided in **Figures A** and **B**.

Part	Dimensions	Quantity
Cut from plywood:		
Box Top	15 x 55 inches	1
Counter Top	31½ x 60½ inches	1
Inner Side	15 x 24¾ inches	2
Shelf	15 x 27 inches	1
Shelf Support	½ x 25 inches	2

Figure A

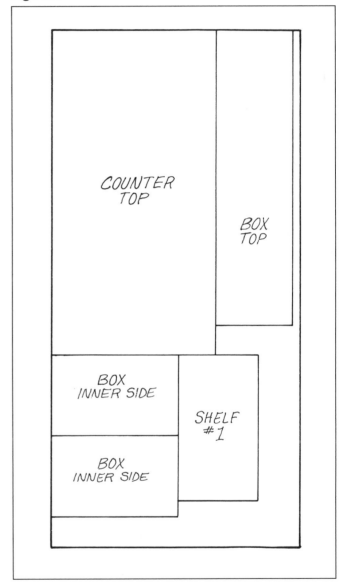

Part	Dimensions	Quantity
Box Front	25¼ x 55½ inches	1
Box Bottom	15 x 55 inches	1
Outer Side	15 x 25¼ inches	2
Divider	15 x 24¾ inches	1
Cut from slat trim:		
Front/Back Trim	61 inches	2
Side Trim	32 inches	2

Figure B

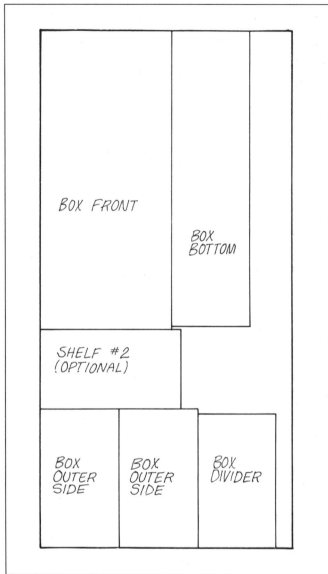

BOX FRONT

BOX BOTTOM

SHELF #2 (OPTIONAL)

BOX OUTER SIDE

BOX OUTER SIDE

BOX DIVIDER

Figure C

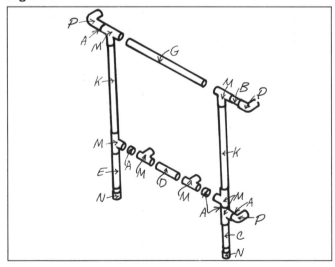

Figure D

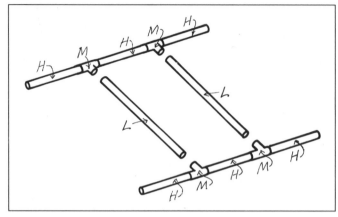

Figure E

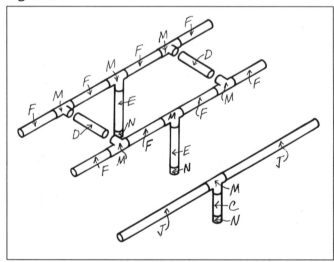

Assembling the frame

The bar frame consists of two identical side sections that are mirror images of each other (**Figure C**), a top support section (**Figure D**), and the bottom support and footrest sections (**Figure E**). The sections are joined together in the final assembly (**Figure F**).

1. One side section is shown in **Figure C**. Begin by assembling, separately, the vertical legs and the lower horizontal portion. Then join these three portions using a **G** piece as the upper horizontal. Finally, assemble and add the front and back extensions as shown.

2. Build a second side section, making it a mirror image of the first. Proceed as you did in step 1, but turn the open ends of all fittings in the opposite direction so they face what will be the center of the bar.

3. The top support section is shown in **Figure D**. Assemble each side portion first, and then join them using the **L** pieces.

4. Refer to **Figure E** as you assemble the bottom support and footrest sections. For the bottom support section, first assemble, separately, the longer portions and lower extensions. Then join them using the **D** pieces. The footrest section is straightforward. Just put the pieces together as shown.

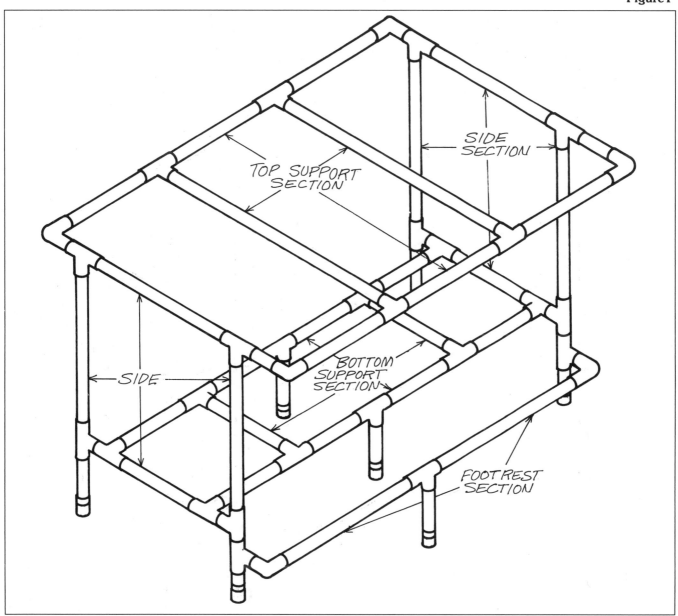

SIDE SECTION

TOP SUPPORT SECTION

SIDE

BOTTOM SUPPORT SECTION

FOOT REST SECTION

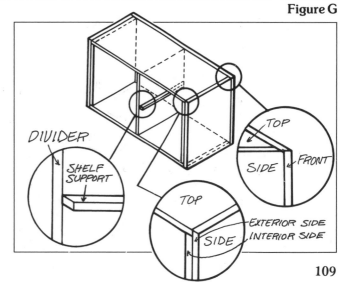

DIVIDER

SHELF SUPPORT

TOP
SIDE FRONT

TOP
SIDE

EXTERIOR SIDE
INTERIOR SIDE

5. Connect all five sections as shown in **Figure F**. You may have to work with the structure a bit to align the fittings so that all the legs are on the ground. If they won't cooperate, pull apart a leg or two and trim the pieces slightly.

Assembling the bar box

The bar box is a 26 x 51 x 14¼-inch plywood box. It can contain as many dividers and shelves as you wish. We have shown only one of each.

1. The box is assembled using simple butt joints, as shown in **Figure G**. First, attach a Shelf Support to one Inner Side piece and to the Divider. You may wish to place the Shelf equally distant from the top and bottom, or closer to the top. In either case, measure carefully the same distance on each piece, so your shelf will be level.

Figure H

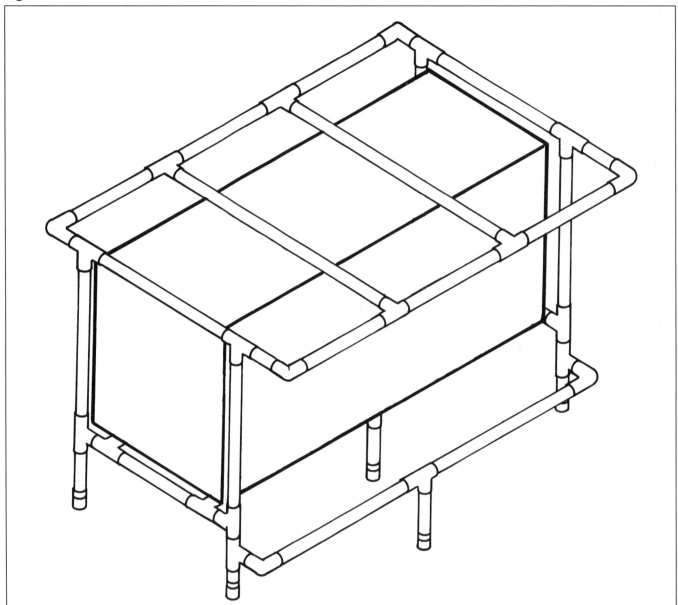

Figure I

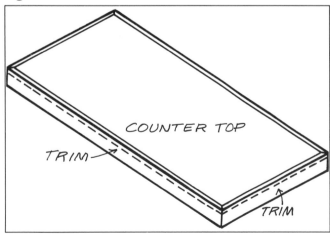

COUNTER TOP

TRIM

TRIM

2. Assemble the box as shown, butting the corners and using glue and nails.

3. Slide the assembled box onto the bottom support section of the frame (**Figure H**), and attach it with screws. (Note: If you wish to use the structure as a workbench rather than a bar, mount the bar box with the open side facing front.)

Adding the counter top

The Counter Top, with Trim pieces attached, is shown in **Figure I**. Miter the ends of the trim pieces for neater corners. The assembled counter top may be placed over the frame, unattached, for easy removal. Or, you may wish to attach it to the frame with screws or molly bolts. If you are going to upholster the counter top, it should be done before the structure is attached to the frame.

Plant Stand & Coffee Table

This structure will hold a host of potted plants, and the low section can be used as a coffee table! It is 75 inches long, 54 inches high at the tall end, and 34 inches deep at the low end. For a sleeker look use glass or acrylic sheet, instead of plywood, for the shelves.

Figure A

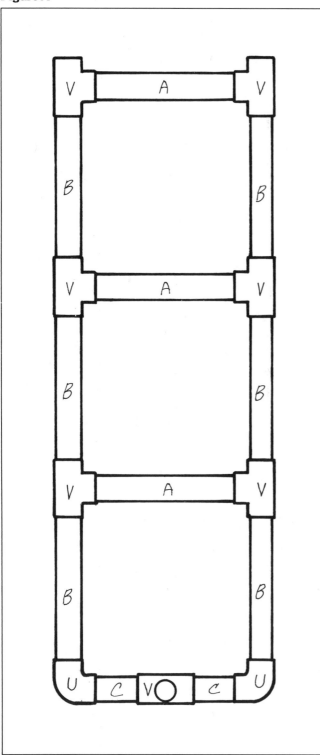

Materials

For the frame:

50 feet of straight 1½-inch PVC pipe.

1½-inch PVC fittings: seventeen 90-degree angle joints, twenty-six T-joints, and two double-T joints.

PVC solvent cement or lots of No. 6 gauge self tapping sheet metal screws, each 1 inch long.

For the shelves:

4 x 4½-foot sheet of ½-inch plywood, waferwood, or the equivalent. If you plan to use the plant stand outdoors, purchase exterior grade material and coat each shelf thoroughly with weatherproofing sealer.

Twenty No. 6 gauge flathead wood screws, each 1 inch long.

Cutting the pipe

The lengths of straight pipe listed below were calculated on the basis of ¾-inch fitting allowances. Check the depth of each fitting and recalculate the lengths of pipe, if necessary, to compensate for the difference on each end. Cut and label the lengths of pipe. Label the fittings as listed.

Part	Length	Quantity
A	10½ inches	8
B	1 foot	14
C	4¼ inches	4
D	6¾ inches	2
E	1⅜ inches	9
F	4 inches	1
G	3¼ inches	1
J	12½ inches	2
K	6½ inches	4
L	11 inches	2
M	12¼ inches	2
N	2⅝ inches	3
P	23⅞ inches	2
Q	21⅞ inches	1
R	18⅜ inches	2
S	19¼ inches	1
T	18 inches	2

Fittings:

U	90-degree joint
V	T-joint
W	Double-T joint

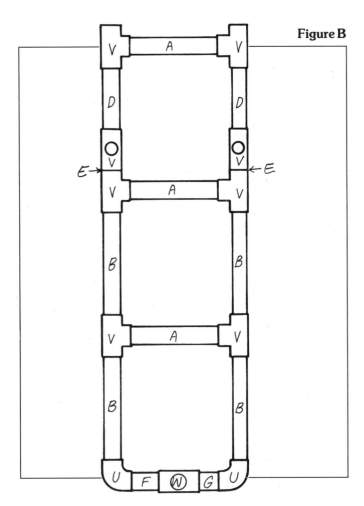

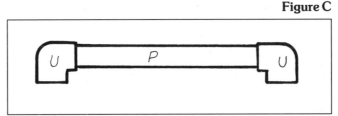

Figure C

Figure D

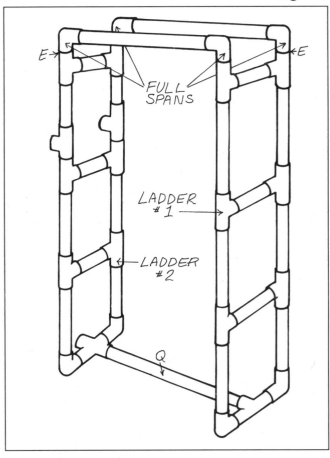

Building the frame

The frame consists of nine sections. Three of these are similar ladder-like assemblies (**Figures A, B,** and **E**). They are connected by two identical full-span sections (**Figure C**), two identical half-span sections (**Figure F**), and crossbars at the bottom. A half-table section (**Figure H**) is joined to the third ladder section. A full-table section (**Figure J**) is connected to the frame with crossbars to form the coffee table. The completed frame is shown in **Figure L**. Because there are so many pieces and fittings, and so many places where the sections must match up perfectly, take special care to make each joint as snug as possible.

1. The first ladder section is shown in **Figure A**. Begin by assembling separately the two vertical portions and the lower horizontal portion. Insert the lower horizontal portion and the three straight **A** pieces into one of the vertical assemblies. Finally, install the remaining vertical portion.

2. The second ladder section is shown in **Figure B**. It is similar to the first one, with a few exceptions. Proceed as you did for the first ladder section. Assemble one vertical portion, using a short **E** piece where indicated to connect the two adjoining **V** fittings near the top. Assemble the remaining vertical portion in the same manner. Assemble the lower horizontal portion and insert it into one of the vertical assemblies. Insert each of the three **A** pieces into the same vertical assembly, and install the remaining vertical portion.

3. Assemble one full-span section, as shown in **Figure C**.

4. Assemble an identical full-span section.

5. Refer to **Figure D** as you join the first two ladder sections, using the full-span sections at the top and the **Q** piece as a crossbar at the bottom. To connect each full-span section, use a short **E** piece at each end. Be sure that the open ends of the **V** fittings near the top of the second ladder section are facing away from the first ladder section.

113

Figure G

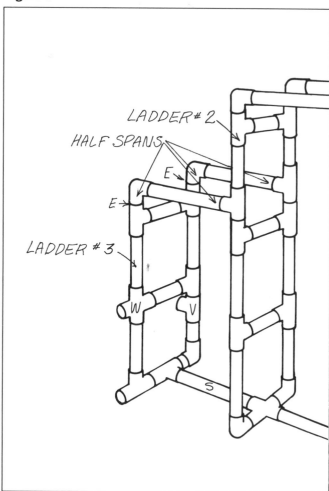

Figure E

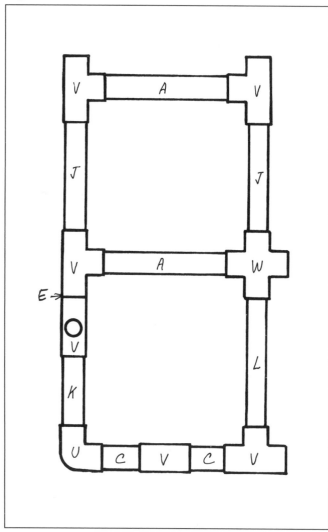

Figure F

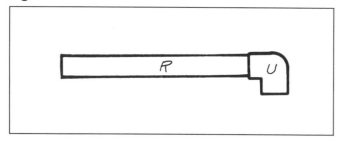

6. The third ladder section is shown in **Figure E**. Begin by assembling the vertical portion on the left side of the drawing, using a short **E** piece where indicated to connect the adjoining **V** fittings. Assemble the lower horizontal portion and insert it into the vertical portion. Insert the two **A** pieces into the vertical portion. Finally, assemble the remaining vertical portion and install it at the opposite side. Be sure that the open ends of all fittings are facing the directions shown.

7. Assemble one half-span section as shown in **Figure** F.

8. Assemble an identical half-span section.

9. Figure G shows the third ladder section connected to the second ladder section. Install it as shown, using the two half-span sections at the top and the **S** piece as a crossbar at the bottom. Be sure to install it as shown, so that the vertical portion with an open **V** fitting near the center is at the back, facing away from the second ladder section. The vertical portion with the **W** fitting should be at the front side.

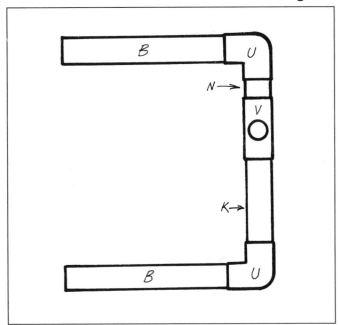

10. Assemble one half-table section as shown in **Figure H**.

11. Connect the half-table section to the third ladder section as shown in **Figure I**. Simply insert the upper and lower **B** pieces of the half-table section into the open **W** and **V** fittings, respectively, at the front of the third ladder section.

12. The full-table section is shown in **Figure J**. Assemble separately the three vertical portions, and then join them using the specified horizontal pieces on each side. Be sure that the open ends of the **V** fittings are facing the direction shown (or not shown, actually, since they are facing away from you).

13. The full-table section is connected to the third ladder and half-table sections as shown in **Figure K**. Use a **T** piece as a crossbar to connect the full-table to the third ladder at the back, and use the remaining **T** piece as a crossbar to connect the full-table to the half-table at the front.

Adding the shelves

Figure L shows the assembled frame with the plywood shelves in place. Refer to this diagram as you work.

1. Cut from plywood one of each of the pieces listed below:

Part	Dimensions
X	19 x 33 inches
Y	12 x 24 inches
Z	12 x 29 inches
AA	12 x 52 inches

2. Part **X** serves as a top for the coffee table portion of the frame. Center it over the pipe. You can secure it by inserting four wood screws down through the plywood into the pipe, or leave it unattached.

3. Part **Y** serves as a shelf on top of the center portion of the frame. Secure it as you did the coffee table top.

Figure I

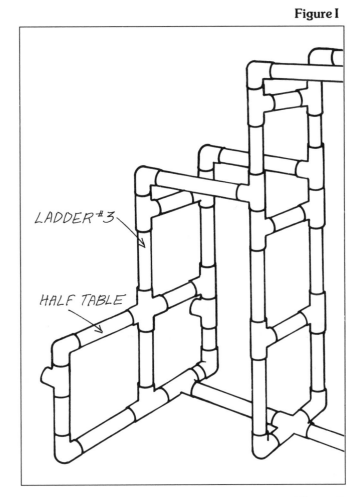

LADDER #3

HALF TABLE

Figure J

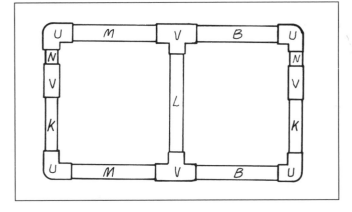

4. Part **Z** serves as a shelf on top of the tallest portion of the frame. If you wish to secure it, use four wood screws.

5. Part **AA** serves as a lower shelf on both the center and tallest portions of the frame. Secure it, if you wish, using the eight remaining wood screws.

Figure K

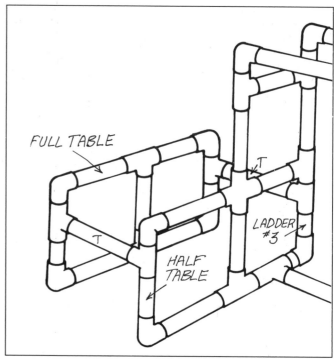

FULL TABLE

T

LADDER #3

HALF TABLE

T

Figure L

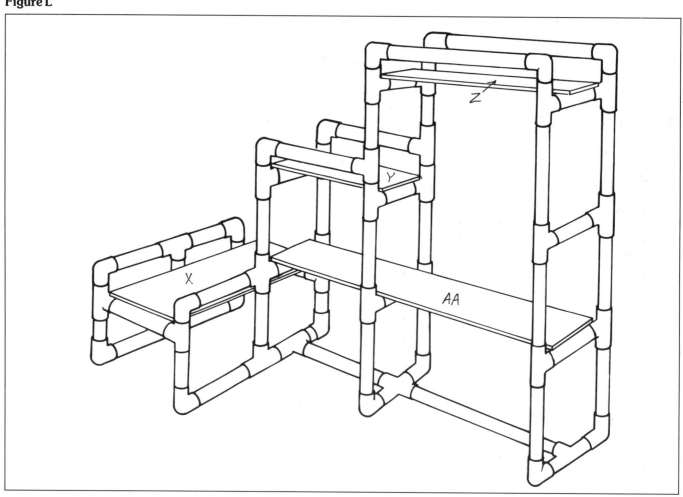

Z

Y

X

AA

Floating Lounge Chair

Good-by water wings, hello life of luxury! This 26 x 55 x 34-inch floating chair is the perfect place to drift and dream away your summer days. The canopy structure is removable, and the chair is attached to the polystyrene float with elastic and fabric straps.

Figure A

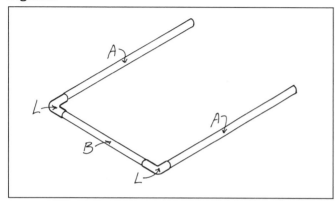

Figure B

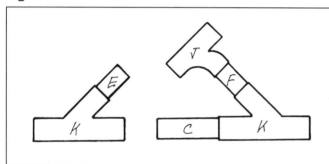

Figure C

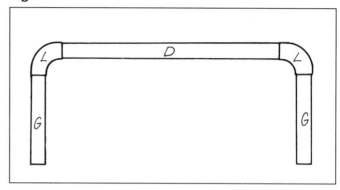

Figure D

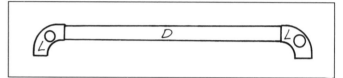

Materials

For the frame:

16 feet of 1½-inch straight PVC pipe.

1½-inch PVC fittings: six 90-degree angle joints, four Y-joints, and two T-joints.

PVC solvent cement or sixty No. 6 gauge self-tapping sheet metal screws, each ¾ or 1 inch long.

9 feet of ¾-inch straight CPVC pipe.

¾-inch CPVC fittings: two 60-degree angle joints and two 90-degree angle joints.

CPVC solvent cement or sixteen No. 6 gauge self-tapping sheet metal screws, each ½ inch long.

For the cover:

3½ yards of 45-inch-wide decorative fabric. We used a heavy cotton duck fabric with a large, tropical print, but any heavy, tightly-woven fabric will work.

23 x 67-inch piece of lightweight cotton fabric for the lining.

4 yards of 36-inch-wide cotton fabric for the float cover.

Two 76-inch lengths of 1-inch-wide heavy elastic.

12-inch-long nylon fastener strip.

Heavy-duty threads to match the fabrics.

118

For the float:

The polystyrene foam float measures 2 feet x 4 feet x 6 inches thick. You can purchase a large block of foam, from which you'll be able to cut several floats this size. A less expensive alternative is to use twelve layers of ½-inch-thick polystyrene foam insulation. You can purchase this material in sheets, and cut 2 x 4-foot pieces. If you opt for this method, use waterproof glue to join the layers.

Building the frame

The chair frame consists of five sections: the seat section (**Figure A**), two identical triangular sections (**Figure B**), the backrest section (**Figure C**), and the lower back section (**Figure D**). The canopy frame is shown in **Figure E**, and the assembled chair and canopy frames are shown in **Figure F**.

1. Cut and label the straight pieces of 1½-inch pipe listed below. The lengths were calculated on the basis of a ¾-inch fitting allowance. Check the depth of each 1½-inch fitting and recalculate the lengths, if necessary, to compensate for the difference on each end. The 1½-inch fittings are listed here with code letters for purposes of identification in the assembly diagrams. Label the fittings also.

Part	Length	Quantity
A	3 feet	2
B	22¼ inches	1
C	5 inches	2
D	21½ inches	2
E	3¼ inches	2
F	2¾ inches	2
G	9¼ inches	2
H	1⅜ inches	2
Fittings:		
J	T-joint	
K	Y-joint	
L	90-degree joint	

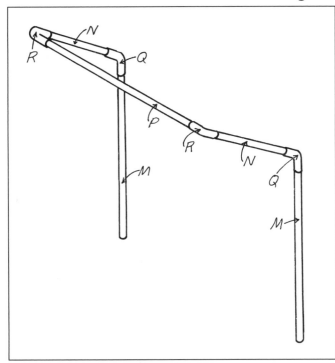

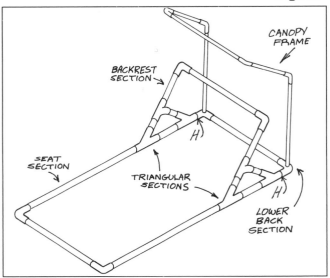

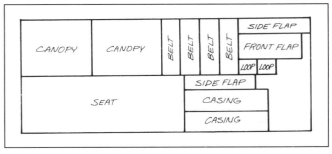

2. Cut and label the lengths of ¾-inch pipe listed below. The lengths were calculated on the basis of 1-inch fitting allowances. Check the depth of each ¾-inch fitting and recalculate the lengths, if necessary, to compensate for the difference on each end. (Note: The **M** pieces are each connected to a fitting on one end only. If it is necessary to recalculate for a different fitting allowance, add or subtract for one end only on these pieces.) The ¾-inch fittings are listed here with code letters for purposes of identification. Label each fitting.

Part	Length	Quantity
M	25 inches	2
N	13 inches	2
P	2 feet	1
Fittings:		
Q	60-degree joint	
R	90-degree joint	

3. Assemble the seat section as shown in **Figure A**.

4. The triangular sections serve as junctions. They connect the seat section to both the backrest and lower back sections. The triangular section is shown in **Figure B**. Assemble the two separate portions and fit them together as shown. Then build an identical triangular section.

5. Assemble one backrest section as shown in **Figure C**.

6. Assemble one lower back section as shown in **Figure D**. Drill a 1-inch-diameter hole through the top of each **L** fitting, to accommodate the ends of the canopy frame. Drill through one side of the fitting only – not all the way through and out the other side.

7. The canopy frame is shown in **Figure E**. Use the ¾-inch pipe and fittings to assemble the frame as shown.

8. The assembled chair and canopy frames are shown in **Figure F**. Join the seat section to one triangular section on each side, but do not use cement or screws yet because the fabric cover must be added first. Add the backrest section. Use a short **H** piece to connect the lower back section to the triangular section on each side. Insert the ends of the canopy frame into the holes in the backrest section.

Making the cover

The chair cover is a lined rectangular piece. A long casing is sewn into each side seam, to accommodate the side bars of the chair frame. Short loops are sewn into the side seams near the top, to accommodate the canopy frame. The fabric belts that hold the chair on the float are added separately, and the elastic strips are added after the cover, frame, and float have been assembled. The canopy is a simple rectangle with flaps sewn into the front and side seams.

1. Cut the pieces listed below from the decorative fabric. A cutting diagram is provided in **Figure G**.

Seat, 23 x 67 inches – cut one
Casings, 8½ x 34 inches – cut two
Loops, 6 x 7½ inches – cut two
Belts, 8 x 22 inches – cut four
Canopy, 22 x 28½ inches – cut two
Side Flaps, 6 x 29 inches – cut two
Front Flap, 10 x 25½ inches – cut one

Figure H

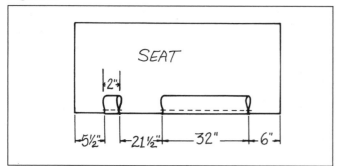

Figure I

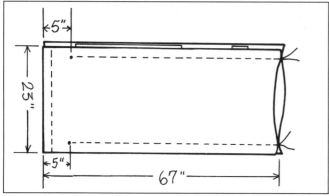

Figure J

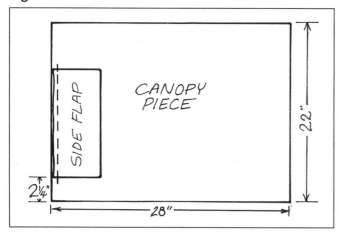

4. Place the Seat piece right side up on a flat surface. Place one stitched casing on top, aligning the long basted edge of the casing with one long side edge of the Seat piece, 6 inches from one end (**Figure H**). Baste the casing in place along the existing line of basting stitches. Place one stitched loop on top of the Seat piece (**Figure H**), aligning the basted edge of the loop with the same long side edge of the Seat piece, 5½ inches from the opposite end. Baste the loop in place. Repeat these procedures to baste the remaining casing and loop to the opposite side edge of the Seat piece.

5. Take the 23 x 67-inch piece of lining fabric and place it right side down on top of the Seat piece. The casings and loops will be sandwiched between. Pin the lining to the Seat piece along all edges. Stitch a 1-inch-wide seam along the bottom short edge (the end nearest the casings). Stitch a 1-inch-wide seam along each side edge, beginning at the top (the end nearest the loop) and ending 5 inches from the bottom (**Figure I**). Leave the top short edge open and unstitched. Stitch these seams again, close to the existing stitching lines, for extra strength.

6. Turn the stitched seat right side out and press the seams flat, pressing the seam allowances in place along the open portion of each side seam. Press the seam allowances to the inside along the open top edge. Topstitch through all thicknesses close to the pressed edges along the open top edge, and again ¼ inch from the first stitching.

7. Fold one Belt piece in half lengthwise, placing right sides together, and pin the two layers along each raw edge. Stitch a 1-inch-wide seam along one short edge and the long edge, leaving the remaining short edge open and unstitched. Clip the corners and turn the stitched belt right side out. Press it flat, placing the seam at one side. Press the seam allowance to the inside along the open edge and whipstitch the pressed edges together. Repeat these procedures to stitch three additional belts, using the remaining Belt pieces.

8. The belts are stitched to the seat in pairs, so that each pair can be wrapped around the polystyrene float and secured together underneath it. Place the seat assembly on a flat surface, lining side up. Place one end of a belt on top of the seat, so that the length of the belt extends out beyond the seat and casing, at a right angle to one side seam. The inner end of the belt should be lapped over the side seam by about 2 inches. Adjust the belt so that it is about 5 inches above the lower end of the casing. Topstitch the belt to the seat, but not to the casing. Stitch a second belt to the seat in the same manner, directly across from the first one. Stitch the remaining two belts to the seat in the same manner, about 5 inches below the upper ends of the casings.

2. On one Casing piece, press a 1-inch-wide hem to the wrong side of the fabric along each short edge only. Stitch the hems in place. Fold the Casing piece in half lengthwise, placing wrong sides together, and run a line of basting stitches ½ inch from the long raw edge. Leave the short edges open. Perform the same procedures on the remaining Casing piece.

3. Fold one Loop piece in half lengthwise, placing right sides together, and stitch a seam 1 inch from the long raw edge. Leave the short edges open and unstitched. Turn the stitched loop right side out and press it flat, placing the seam at one side. Topstitch through all thicknesses, ¼ inch from the seamed edge. Fold the stitched loop in half widthwise and run a line of basting stitches ½ inch from the short raw edge. Perform the same procedures on the remaining Loop piece.

Hammock, page 38

Patio & Game Room Bar, page 106

Plant Stand, page 111

Parson's Table, page 34

Bird Castle, page 53

Chaise Lounge, page 80

Bookcase, page 92

Sling Chair, page 133

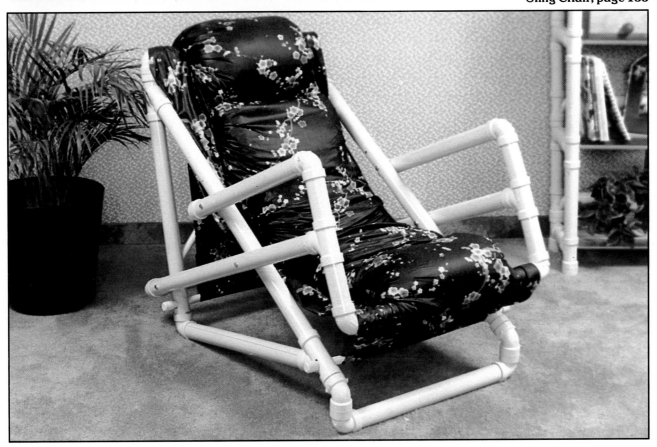

Coat Rack, page 146

Yard Swing, page 27

Floating
Lounge Chair, page 117

Lawn & Garden Cart, page 59

Picnic Table, page 31

Making the canopy

1. The canopy is assembled very much like the seat, with the flaps sewn into the seams. First, prepare the flaps. Fold one Side Flap piece in half widthwise, placing right sides together. Pin the layers together along each raw edge. Stitch a 1-inch-wide seam along the short edge and one long edge, leaving the remaining long edge open and unstitched. Clip the corners, turn the stitched flap right side out, and press. Run a line of basting stitches ½ inch from the long open edges. Topstitch through all thicknesses ¼ inch from each short edge and from the long edge that is not basted. Repeat these procedures to prepare the remaining Side Flap piece.

2. Fold the Front Flap piece in half lengthwise, placing right sides together, and pin the layers together along each raw edge. Stitch a 1-inch-wide seam along each short edge, leaving the long raw edge open and unstitched. Clip the corners, turn the stitched flap right side out, and press. Run a line of basting stitches ½ inch from the open long edge. Topstitch through all thicknesses ¼ inch from each short edge and from the long edge that is not basted.

3. Place one Canopy piece right side up on a flat surface. Place one of the stitched side flaps on top, aligning the basted raw edge of the flap with one short edge of the Canopy piece (**Figure J**). The flap should be 2¼ inches from one long edge of the Canopy piece. Baste the flap in place along the existing line of basting stitches. Baste the remaining side flap to the opposite edge of the Canopy piece in the same manner.

4. Place the stitched front flap on top of the Canopy piece, aligning the basted raw edge of the flap with the long edge of the Canopy piece that is closest to the side flaps. Center the flap between the side edges. Baste it in place as you did the side flaps.

5. Pin the remaining Canopy piece right side down on top of the first piece. (The flaps will be sandwiched between.) Stitch a 1-inch-wide seam along each edge that includes a flap, leaving the remaining long edge open and unstitched. Clip the corners, turn the canopy right side out, and press.

6. Press a ½-inch-wide hem to the wrong side of the fabric all the way around the open raw edge. Repeat this procedure so that you have a double-turned hem ½ inch wide. Machine stitch the hem. On the same edge, press a 2½-inch-wide hem to the wrong side of the fabric. Machine stitch this hem, and then topstitch ¼ inch from the hemmed edge.

Installing the covers

1. To install the chair cover, first completely disassemble the seat section of the chair frame. (See **Figures A** and **F** to refresh your memory.) Insert the **B** piece through the casing at the bottom of the chair cover. Insert one of the **A** pieces through the casing on one side of the cover, and insert the other **A** piece through the casing on the opposite side. Reassemble the seat section and reinstall it on the frame.

2. Drape the upper end of the cover over the top crossbar of the backrest section. Pull the upper end of the cover downward until it is tight, and pin it to the wrong side of the cover. To secure it, proceed in one of two ways. You can stitch the upper end to the cover by hand, using heavy-duty thread and

stitching back and forth several times for extra strength. Machine stitching will be more secure, but to do this you'll have to mark the position on the cover where the upper end should be attached, remove the cover from the frame (repeating in reverse order the procedures in step 1), and stitch the end securely to the cover. To replace the cover, disassemble the backrest section, insert the **D** piece through the wide casing at the upper end of the cover, reassemble and reinstall the backrest section, and repeat the necessary procedures to reassemble and reinstall the seat section.

3. You'll be happy to hear that the canopy cover is easy to install. You simply slip it over the canopy frame. The loops at the top of the chair cover will help secure the canopy frame. Remove the entire canopy frame from the chair frame, slip the ends of the pipes through the loops in the chair cover, and reinstall the canopy frame.

Making the float

1. Cut a piece of solid polystyrene foam, 2 x 4 feet and 6 inches thick. (Or, cut twelve pieces of ½-inch-thick foam insulation, each 2 x 4 feet, and glue them together.)

2. Cut two pieces of lightweight cotton fabric for the float cover, each 32 x 68 inches.

3. Place the fabric pieces right sides together and stitch a ¾-inch-wide seam along each long edge. Stitch the seams again for extra strength. Press the seams open and turn the cover right side out.

4. Insert the foam float inside the cover, placing the seams at the centers of the sides. Center the float between the open ends of the cover.

5. Fold the ends of the fabric as you would wrapping paper at the ends of a gift, and pin them in place. Hand stitch the end flaps closed.

Attaching the float

The float is attached to the chair with the four fabric belts and two elastic strips.

1. Place the assembled chair on top of the float and wrap the belts around to the bottom. Attach nylon fastener strips to each pair of belts so that they hold the chair firmly in place.

2. The elastic strips serve to secure the chair and float lengthwise, as the belts do widthwise. Wrap an elastic strip around one end of the crossbar at the foot of the chair. Stitch the end of the elastic to the strip to secure it. Pull the opposite end of the strip underneath the float and up to the crossbar at the head of the chair. Wrap it around this crossbar and secure it. Attach the remaining elastic strip in the same manner, on the opposite end of each crossbar.

Serving Cart

Whether it be tea on the veranda or potted plants in the garage you can serve in style with this project. Overall dimensions are 37 inches tall x 18 inches wide x 40 inches long. You'll find this to be one of the handiest items around the house. When your spouse discovers it, you may need two.

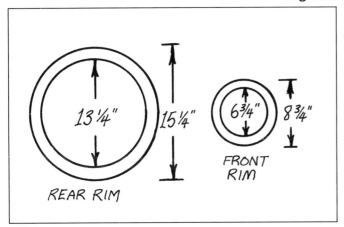

Figure A

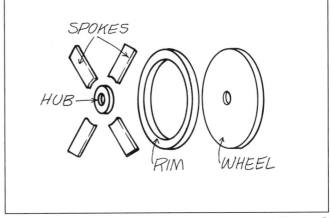

Figure B

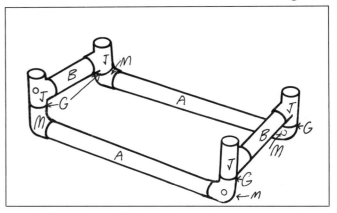

Figure C

Materials

20 feet of straight 1½-inch PVC pipe.

4 feet of straight ¾-inch PVC pipe.

1½-inch PVC fittings: eight 90-degree angle joints, eight T-joints, and two 45-degree angle joints.

¾-inch PVC fittings: four end caps.

PVC solvent cement or a handful of No. 6 gauge self-tapping sheet metal screws, each 1 inch long.

4 x 4-foot sheet of ½-inch plywood.

Cutting the pipe

1. The required lengths of straight 1½-inch pipe listed below were calculated on the basis of ⅝-inch fitting allowances. Check the depth of each fitting and, if necessary, recalculate the length of each straight piece of pipe to compensate for the difference on each end. Cut and label the straight pieces of 1½-inch pipe listed below.

Part	Length	Quantity
A	26 inches	2
B	12¼ inches	2
C	25¼ inches	2
D	12¾ inches	2
E	3¼ inches	2
F	19 inches	4
G	1⅛ inches	8

2. Cut and label the straight pieces of ¾-inch pipe listed below. There is no need to recalculate to compensate for fitting allowances.

Part	Length	Quantity
H	21 inches	2

3. The fittings will be labeled as listed below.

Part	Description
J	T-joint
K	End cap
L	45-degree joint
M	90-degree joint

Cutting the plywood

The plywood pieces required for the wheels and counter surfaces are listed below. Cut the pieces as listed.

Part	Dimensions	Quantity
Rear Wheel	15¼ inch diameter	2
Rear Rim	See Figure A	2
Rear Spokes	1 x 4⅞ inches	8
Rear Hub	3½ inch diameter	2
Front Wheel	8¾ inch diameter	2
Front Rim	See Figure A	2
Front Spokes	½ x 2 inches	8
Front Hub	2¾ inch diameter	2
Upper Counter	17 x 26 inches	1
Lower Counter	12½ x 30 inches	1

Wheel assembly

1. The wheel assembly is shown in **Figure B**. Contour both ends of each Rear and Front Spoke, as shown, so they will fit flush against the Rear and Front Hubs and Rims respectively.

2. Refer to the wheel assembly detail in **Figure B**. To make each wheel, glue the Hub, four Spokes, and Rim to the solid Wheel. Clamp, and allow the assembly to dry completely.

3. Drill a ⅞-inch hole through the exact center of each assembled wheel.

131

Figure D

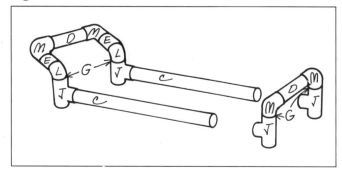

Figure E

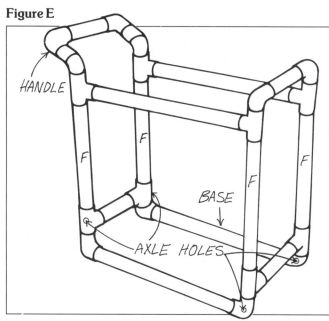

HANDLE
F
F
F
F
BASE
AXLE HOLES

Figure F

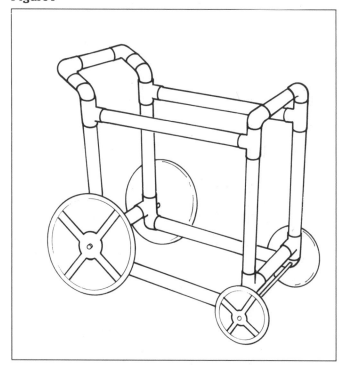

Figure G

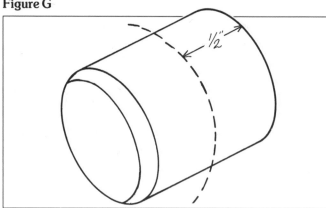

½"

Assembling the frame

The cart frame consists of the base section (**Figure C**), the handle section (**Figure D**), and four connecting pieces (**Figure E**). The assembled cart, complete with axles and wheels, is shown in **Figure F**.

1. Refer to **Figure C** as you assemble the base section. Start with one side **A** piece and connect the fittings as shown. The **M** and **J** fittings are joined using the short **G** pieces. (The **G** pieces will be covered completely by the fittings.) Now connect the two side portions using the **B** pieces.

2. Refer to **Figure D** as you assemble the handle section. Start with one side **C** piece and connect the fittings as shown. Use the **E** pieces between the **L** and **M** fittings at the top of the handle, then connect the two side portions with the **D** pieces.

3. Refer to **Figure E** as you bring the base and handle sections together using the **F** pieces.

Wheel to frame assembly

1. You are now ready to drill the axle holes (**Figure E**). Measure your drilling points to the center of the fittings carefully so the axles will be level and parallel. Drill a 1-inch hole through both sides of each **M** fitting at the front of the base section. The axle will be exposed and parallel to the **B** piece above it. Drill a hole through the center of each **J** fitting at the back of the base section. This axle will pass, hidden, through the **B** piece.

2. Now take the four end caps (**K**) and cut through each one, ½ inch from the open end (**Figure G**). This will give you four PVC "washers" and four "short caps" with which to secure the wheels.

3. The **H** pieces serve as the axles. Slide one **H** piece through the axle holes at the front of the frame, making sure it turns freely in the holes and does not bind. Insert the remaining **H** piece through the holes in the back.

4. On the end of one **H** piece mount a washer, an assembled wheel, and a shortened end cap (**K**). Slide the wheel and washer out until the wheel is sandwiched between the **K** fitting and the washer. Cement the cap and washer in place. Repeat this process for each wheel.

Counter Surfaces

Attach the counter surfaces to the frame using screws.

Sling Chair

We've renamed this little darlin' the "Ahhhhhh Chair." The only problem you'll have with it is ousting visitors who are too comfortable to move. The stuffed sling can be removed easily for cleaning. Overall dimensions of the chair are 28 x 33 x 42 inches.

Figure A

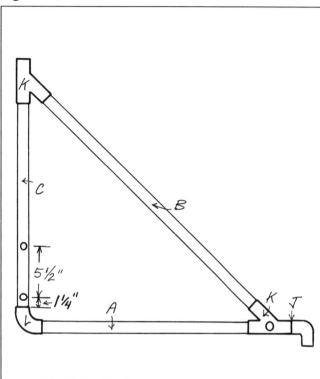

Figure B

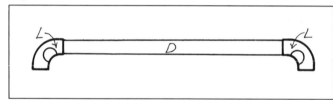

Materials

For the frame:

34 feet of straight 1½-inch PVC pipe.

1½-inch PVC fittings: fourteen 90-degree angle joints, four
   Y-joints, two T-joints, and two end caps.

11 feet of straight ¾-inch CPVC pipe.

¾-inch CPVC fittings: four end caps, and one double-T joint.
   (We didn't have a double-T in this size, so we made one
   from a regular T-joint and an end cap.)

PVC solvent cement, or about 100 No. 6 gauge self-tapping
   sheet metal screws, each 1 inch long.

CPVC solvent cement.

Six hex-head machine bolts, each 4 inches long and ⅜ inch
   in diameter with a cap nut to fit.

For the sling:

6¼ yards of medium-weight decorative fabric, at least 40 inches wide. (We used polished cotton.)

Five bags of polyester fiberfill.

Thread to match the fabric.

Figure C

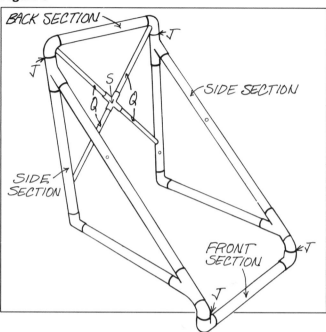

Cutting the pipe

1. The lengths of 1½-inch pipe listed below were calculated on the basis of ¾-inch fitting allowances. Check the
depth of each 1½-inch fitting and recalculate each length, if
necessary, to compensate for the difference on each end. Cut
and label the lengths of straight pipe. Label each fitting with
the code letter listed.

Part	Length	Quantity
A	25 inches	2
B	35⅜ inches	2
C	24⅛ inches	2
D	20½ inches	2
E	21½ inches	2
F	5⅜ inches	4
G	23½ inches	2
H	36¼ inches	2
J	1⅜ inches	6
Fittings:		
K	Y-joint	
L	90-degree joint	
M	End cap	
N	T-joint	

2. Cut and label the lengths of ¾-inch pipe listed below.
There's no need to recalculate for fitting allowances. Label
the fittings as listed.

Part	Length	Quantity
P	26 inches	2
Q	17 inches	4
Fittings:		
R	End cap	
S	Double T-joint	

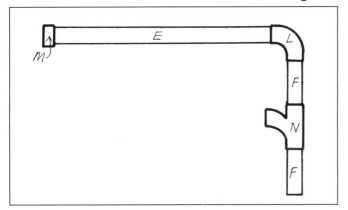

Assembling the frame

There are two separate assemblies that form the frame: the seat assembly and the arm assembly. The seat assembly consists of five sections: two identical side sections (**Figure A**), identical back and front sections (**Figure B**), and a criss-cross brace section that is shown on the completed seat assembly in **Figure C**. The arm assembly consists of four sections: two identical armrest sections (**Figure D**), a back support section (**Figure E**), and a front section that is identical to the front and back sections of the seat assembly. The completed arm assembly is shown in **Figure F**. In the final step, the arm and seat assemblies are bolted together as shown in **Figure G**.

Building the seat assembly

1. Assemble one side section as shown in **Figure A**. Use a short **J** piece to connect the **K** and **L** fittings shown on the lower right-hand portion of the drawing.

2. The side section is drilled in two places to accommodate the rods that will hold the fabric sling in place. Drill a 1-inch-diameter hole through the lower **K** fitting where indicated, in one side and out the other. Drill in as straight a line as possible, or you'll be sorry when you try to insert the rod. Drill another 1-inch hole through the vertical **C** piece, 1¼ inches above the fitting. Again, drill in one side and out the other in as straight a line as possible.

3. The side section is also drilled to accommodate the criss-cross brace section. Drill a 1-inch hole into the **C** piece, 5½ inches above the lower hole that you just drilled (**Figure A**). Drill through one side of the pipe only. The brace pipe will be inserted at an angle, so enlarge the hole lengthwise until it measures about 1⅜ inches from top to bottom.

4. Repeat the procedures in steps 1, 2, and 3 to form an identical side section. Be extremely careful to align the holes you drill with the ones in the first section.

5. Assemble the front section as shown in **Figure B**.

6. Assemble an identical back section (**Figure B**).

7. The back section only must be drilled to accommodate the upper ends of the criss-cross brace section. Drill a 1-inch hole into each **L** fitting, in the exact center of the inside corner angle. Do not drill all the way through the fitting and out the other side.

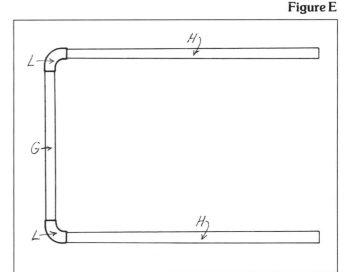

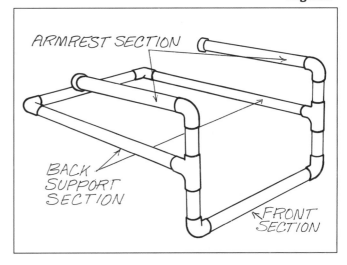

ARMREST SECTION

BACK SUPPORT SECTION

FRONT SECTION

8. The sections that you have built are joined together with the criss-cross braces to form the seat assembly (**Figure C**). First, assemble the braces by inserting the four **Q** pieces into the openings of the **S** fitting. To begin the seat assembly, place the two triangular side sections side by side, with the elongated holes facing center. Insert the criss-cross brace as shown. Insert a short **J** piece into the open fitting at the top of each side section, and install the back section on top. If the brace section is too long or too wide to allow the back section to fit properly, trim the straight braces a little at a time to make sure you don't overcompensate. Finally, insert a short **J** piece into the **L** fitting at each end of the front section, and install this section where indicated.

135

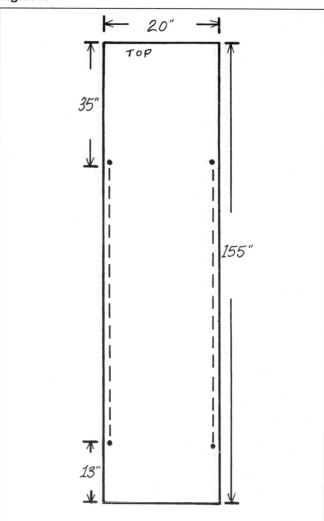

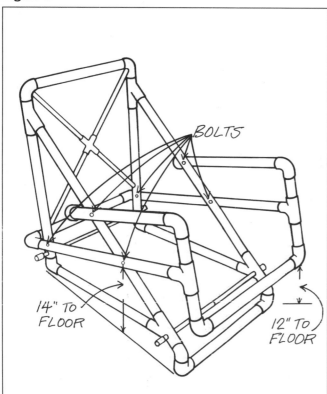

Building the arm assembly

1. Assemble one armrest section as shown in **Figure D**.

2. Assemble an identical armrest section.

3. Assemble the back support section (**Figure E**).

4. The front section is identical to the back and front sections of the seat assembly (**Figure B**), but it is slightly longer. Substitute a **G** piece for the **D** piece shown in **Figure B**.

5. The completed arm assembly is shown in **Figure F**. Insert one end of the back section into the open **N** fitting in each armrest section, and install the front section at the bottom.

Final frame assembly

The assembled frame is shown in **Figure G**. An assistant will be most helpful during this stage of the game. The seat and arm assemblies are bolted together in three places on

each side, as shown. Slip the arm assembly down over the seat assembly. The back section of the arm assembly should be about 1 inch above the holes that will house the rear sling rod, and it should extend about 2 inches beyond the back of the seat assembly. Tilt the front of the arm assembly upward as shown. Mark the positions for the bolt holes in both assemblies, and drill the holes. Reposition the two assemblies, insert the bolts from the outside in, and fasten each with a cap nut on the inside.

Making the sling

1. Cut the following pieces from the decorative fabric:

    Front Sling, 20 x 155 inches – cut one

    Back Sling, 20 x 105 inches – cut one

    Flap, 13 x 65 inches – cut two

2. The Front Sling piece is gathered lengthwise so that it matches the length of the Back Sling piece. Run a line of basting stitches ½ inch from each long edge of the Front Sling piece, beginning 35 inches from one end (this will be the top) and ending 13 inches from the opposite end (**Figure H**). Pull the threads to form even gathers until each side measures

Figure I

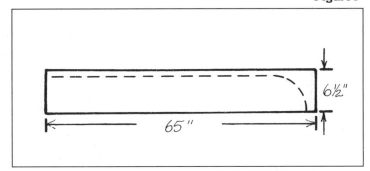

6½"

65"

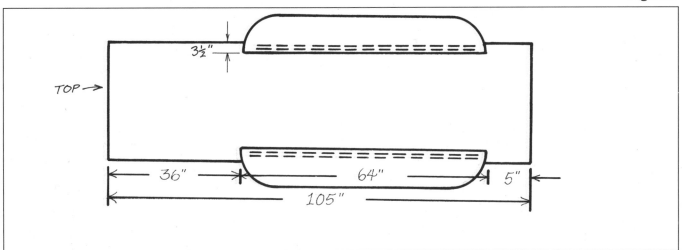

3½"

TOP →

36"   64"   5"

105"

105 inches from top to bottom. Tie off the threads and run a line of short stitches over each line of basting stitches to secure the gathers in place.

3. On the finished sling, a flap will extend out from each side to cover the space between the cushioned portion and the chair frame. To make a flap, fold one Flap piece in half lengthwise, placing right sides together. Pin the raw edges together along the long edge and one short edge. Stitch a ½-inch-wide seam along the long edge, and then angle the stitching across one short edge as shown in **Figure I**. Leave the remaining short edge open and unstitched.

4. Trim the seam allowances along the curved portion of the seam, clip the curve, turn the stitched flap right side out, and press. Turn the open raw edges of the flap to the inside, angling the edge as you did the other short edge. Press, and whipstitch the opening edges together.

5. Repeat the procedures in steps 3 and 4 to form an identical flap, using the remaining Flap piece.

6. Place the Back Sling piece right side up on a flat surface. Place the two stitched flaps on top, positioning them where indicated in **Figure J**. Pin each flap to the Back Sling piece along the long straight edge of the flap, and stitch close to this edge, through all thicknesses. Stitch again, ¼ inch from the first stitching line.

7. The flaps will extend out from the finished sling as shown in **Figure J**. For the time being, fold each flap in toward the center and pin it in place, so it won't get caught when you stitch the side seams.

8. Place the gathered Front Sling piece, right side down, on top of the Back Sling piece. Be sure that the pieces are turned so that the top and bottom edges of each are aligned. The flaps will be sandwiched between. Stitch a ½-inch-wide

137

Figure L

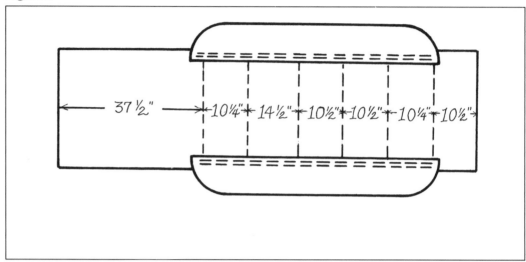

Figure K

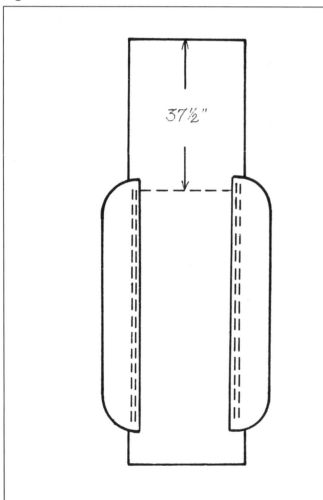

seam along each long edge and along the short edge that is farthest from the flaps. (This will be the top end of the sling.) Leave the remaining short edge open and unstitched. Clip the corners and turn the stitched sling right side out. Press the seam allowances to the inside along the open edge, but do not stitch them together yet. Remove the pins that are holding the flaps.

Stuffing the sling

We used five bags of polyfill to stuff the sling, and divided the sling into five sections so the stuffing wouldn't all end up at the bottom. To keep the sling puffier, and to make it more ahhhhh-inspiring, we left the stuffing in the plastic bags. The only drawback to this is the slight crackling sound that emanates when someone sits down, but that doesn't seem to have disturbed anyone. Whether you prefer to leave the stuffing in the bags or take it out, work with one bag at a time as you stuff the sling.

1. First, stitch across the sling between the flaps, through the Front and Back pieces, 37¼ inches from the top end (**Figure K**).

2. Stuff one bag of polyfill into the sling through the open lower end, and push it all the way up to the stitching line. Stitch across the sling again, below the bag of stuffing, in the same manner as you did in step 1. This stitching line should be approximately 10¼ inches from the first stitching line.

3. Repeat the procedures in step 2 as you stuff each of the remaining bags of polyfill into the sling. Place the stitching lines that divide the sections as shown in **Figure L**. Don't worry if your stitching lines curve slightly. It's almost impossible to make them straight because of the bulky stuffing. Just begin and end each line at the distance shown, and allow the line to curve slightly in the center.

138

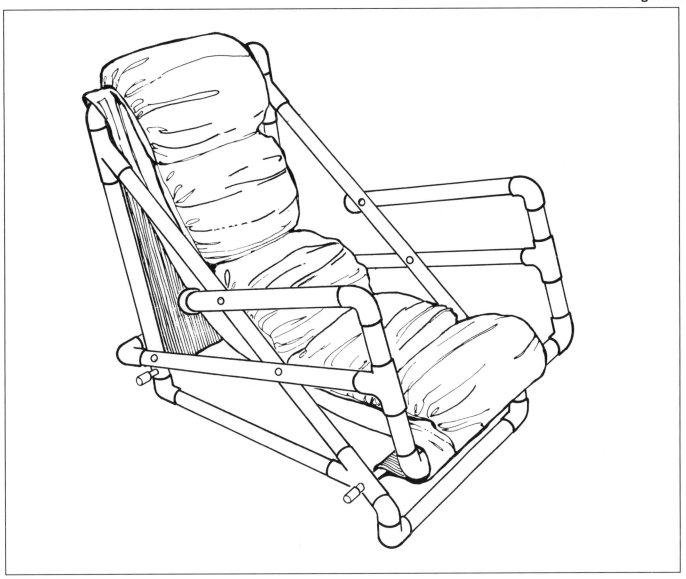

4. Whipstitch the lower open edges of the sling together. Fold this whipstitched edge to the back of the sling, forming a 2½-inch-wide hem. Machine stitch the hem in place, close to the whipstitched edge. Stitch again, ¼ inch from the first stitching. The casing thus formed will house the pipe that holds the lower end of the sling in place on the frame.

5. To make a similar casing at the opposite end of the sling, fold the upper edge to the back, forming a 9-inch-wide hem. Stitch as you did the lower casing.

Installing the sling

The assembled chair, with the sling in place, is shown in **Figure M**. As you install the sling, be sure that the flat side will be at the back and the gathered side will be at the front.

1. You should have two lengths of ¾-inch pipe left over from the frame assembly (the two **P** pieces). Insert one of these pieces through the holes in one side of the frame, near the front end (**Figure M**). Slide the pipe through the casing at the lower end of the sling, and continue to push it on through the holes in the opposite side of the frame. Leave equal extensions on each side of the frame, and install an end cap (**R** fitting) on each end of the pipe.

2. Insert the remaining pipe through the holes in one side of the frame near the back. Pull the upper end of the sling around the outside of the front crossbar on the arm assembly. Drape it over the top crossbar at the back of the frame, and pull it down to the bottom, inside the back crossbar of the arm assembly. Insert the pipe through the casing and push it on through the holes in the opposite side of the frame. Secure it with end caps. The sling should not be taut.

139

Coffee Table

Need a coffee table you can put your feet up on? Try this 20 x 42 x 17-inch model. The top can be made of anything you like, in any size. How about plywood for the game room, glass or clear plastic for the living room, or planking to match your patio or deck.

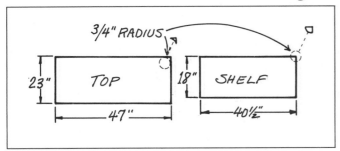

Materials

14 feet of straight 1½-inch PVC pipe.

9 feet of straight ¾-inch PVC pipe.

1½-inch PVC fittings: four 90-degree angle joints.

¾-inch PVC fittings: four end caps.

PVC solvent cement or a handful of No. 6 gauge self-tapping sheet metal screws, each 1 inch long.

40½ x 18-inch piece of ¼-inch plywood.

Tabletop: The minimum size is 23 x 47 inches, but you may prefer a larger surface. We suggest ½-inch lumber core plywood (baltic birch or one of the more attractive woods), or ¼-inch glass or plastic. If you use glass, have the edges beveled and the corners rounded when cut.

Fasteners: To attach the tabletop to the frame, use wood screws for plywood or planking, or strong double-sided tape for plastic or glass. You can also use nylon fastener strips, attached to the tabletop and frame with epoxy glue, if you want a removable top.

Cutting the pipe

1. The required lengths of straight pipe listed below were calculated on the basis of ⅝-inch fitting allowances. Check the depth of each fitting and, if necessary, recalculate the length of each straight piece of pipe to compensate for the difference on each end. Cut and label the straight pieces of 1½-inch pipe listed below.

Part	Length	Quantity
A	37¾ inches	2
B	15¾ inches	2
C	14½ inches	4

2. Cut and label the straight pieces of ¾-inch pipe listed below. It is not necessary to recalculate.

Part	Length	Quantity
D	40¾ inches	2
E	16¾ inches	2

3. Label the fittings as listed below.

Part	Description
F	90-degree angle joint
G	End cap

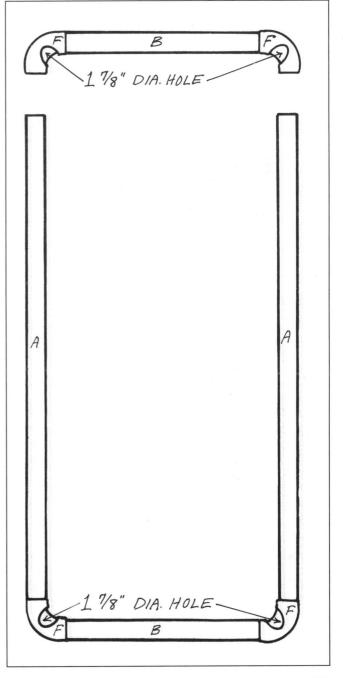

Figure C

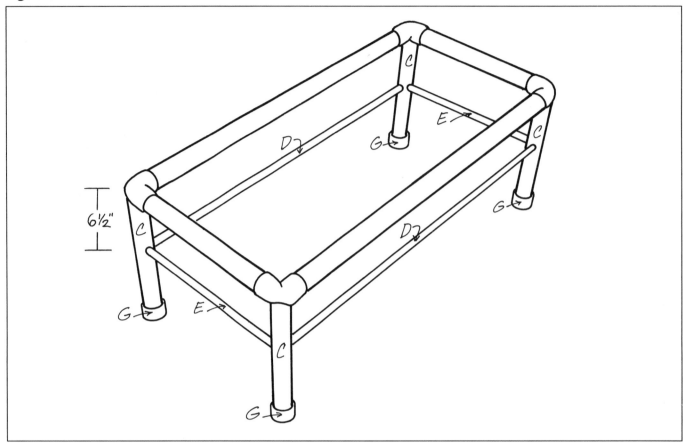

The top and shelf

Refer to **Figure A** for the dimensions of the Top and Shelf. For the Top we used ¼-inch plate glass (you can use anything you like). The glass company cut it to our specifications, beveled the edges, and rounded the corners (¾-inch radius) so all we had to do was fasten it down at the corners. (Pretty slick, huh?) For the Shelf we used ¼-inch plywood. The Shelf actually serves two purposes: it functions as a shelf (surprise) and it adds to the stability of the table. The corners of the Shelf are cut away (a ¾-inch radius) to fit around the table legs.

Frame assembly

The table frame consists of the surface section (**Figure B**), and four legs with connecting pieces (**Figure C**).

1. Refer to **Figure B** as you assemble the surface section. Join the two **A** pieces and two **B** pieces using the four **F** fittings as shown.

2. Place the assembled surface section on a flat surface and drill a 1⅞-inch hole straight down into each of the four **F** fittings. Drill only through one side of each fitting — not all the way through and out the other side.

3. Measure 6½ inches from the top of one **C** piece, (**Figure C**), and drill a 1-inch hole through one side. Turn the pipe

one-quarter turn and drill another hole. Repeat this process for all four **C** pieces.

4. Connect two **C** pieces by inserting an **E** piece into opposing holes drilled in step 3. Make sure that the remaining two holes in the **C** pieces both point toward the center of the table (**Figure C**). Repeat this process so that you have two pairs of legs (**C** pieces) that are mirror images of one another.

5. Insert two **D** pieces in the remaining holes of *one pair* of **C** pieces. Do not connect all four **C** pieces yet as you will not be able to install the shelf.

6. Place the shelf over the two **D** pieces, butting the inletted corners against the **C** pieces.

7. Install the remaining pair of **C** pieces. The shelf will extend over the **E** pieces and butt against all four **C** pieces.

8. Insert the tops of the **C** pieces into the holes drilled in the **F** fittings of the surface section.

9. Attach end caps (**G**) onto the ends of the **C** pieces.

Adding the tabletop

The last step in completing the Coffee Table is to center and attach your selected top. The method of attaching the Top to the frame will depend on the material you chose, but here are a few suggestions: glue, wood screws, decorative brass screws, nylon fastener strips. The list can be as varied as your choice of materials.

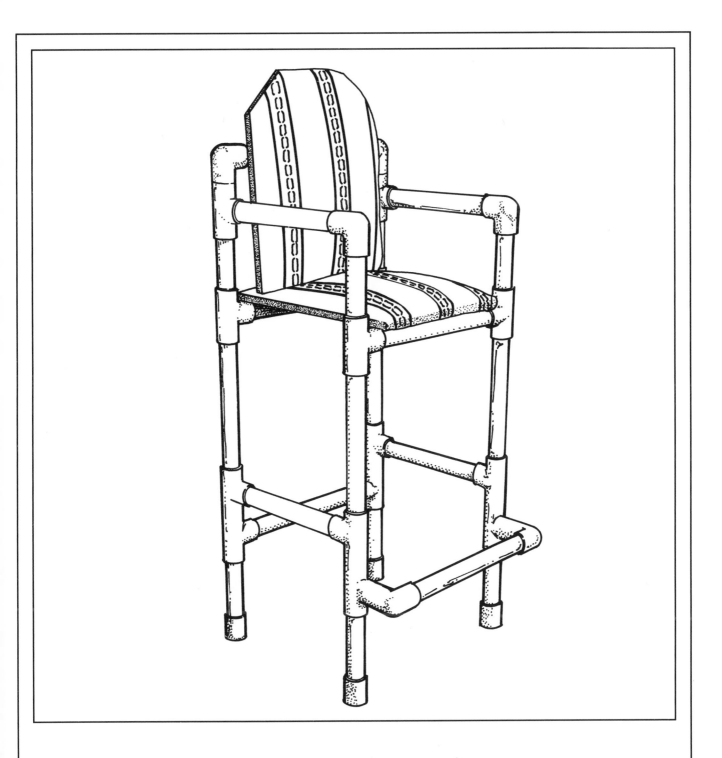

Bar Stool

Mosey on up to the kitchen counter and have a seat on this Texas-size bar stool. The overall dimensions are 45 x 21 x 18 inches. The height of the plywood seat can be adjusted quite easily by altering the length of the legs.

Figure A

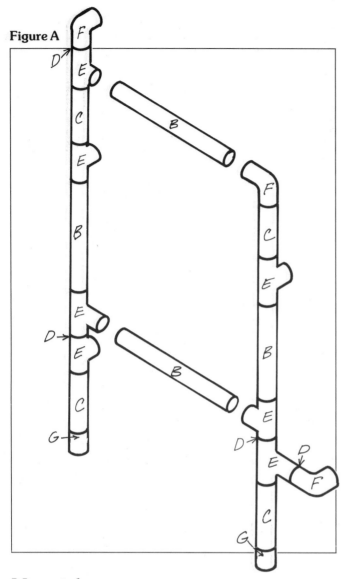

Figure B

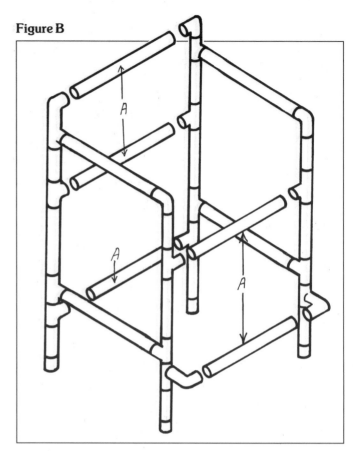

Part	Length	Quantity
A	16⅝ inches	5
B	13⅝ inches	8
C	6½ inches	8
D	1⅞ inches	8

Fittings:

E	T-joint	
F	90-degree joint	
G	End cap	

Materials

24 feet of straight 1¼-inch PVC pipe.

1¼-inch PVC fittings: fourteen T-joints, six 90-degree angle joints, and four end caps.

PVC solvent cement or a large handful of No. 6 gauge self-tapping sheet metal screws, each ½ inch long.

Six molly bolts, each long enough to accommodate a "wall" ⅝ inch thick.

Four flathead wood screws, each 1 inch long.

Two pieces of ¾-inch plywood or waferwood, each 14½ x 18¼ inches, for the seat and seat back.

Scrap of solid wood, ¾ x ¾ x 14½ inches.

Cutting the pipe

The required lengths of straight pipe listed at right were calculated on the basis of 1-inch-long fitting allowances. Check the depth of each fitting and, if necessary, recalculate the length of each straight piece of pipe to compensate for the difference on each end. Cut and label the straight pieces of pipe. Label the fittings with their code letters, for purposes of identification in the assembly process.

Frame assembly

The bar stool frame consists of two identical side sections (**Figure A**) that are mirror images of each other. The side sections are joined by five crossbars in the final assembly step (**Figure B**).

1. Refer to **Figure A** as you assemble one side section. To avoid trouble, assemble the vertical front and back legs first, and then connect them with the **B** pieces as shown. The short **D** pieces will be covered completely by the fittings they join.

2. Make a second side section identical to the first, but turn the open ends of the **E** and **F** fittings so that the two side sections are mirror images of each other.

3. Join the two sides using the five straight **A** pieces, as shown in **Figure B**.

4. When you have achieved a good fit all around, perform the final assembly. Cement the joints or secure each with two self-tapping screws. Proceed in the same order in which you did the dry assembly.

Figure C

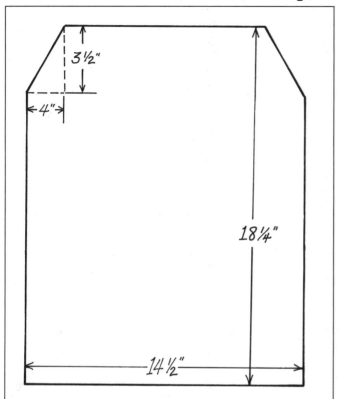

Adding the wooden seat

1. The two plywood rectangles will serve as the Seat and Seat Back. Cut off the corners at the upper end of the Seat Back (**Figure C**). We used a cove bit to rout the edges on one side of each piece. The routed edges will be on the front of the Seat Back, and on the top of the Seat.

2. This step is optional. If you wish to upholster the bar stool instead of making or buying cushions, it is easily done. Cut a piece of 1- or 2-inch-thick foam rubber to match each plywood piece and glue it in place. Place a piece of fabric on top of the foam, wrap the edges around to the back and staple the edges in place. Cut an additional piece of fabric, 1 inch larger than the Back on all edges. Fold the 1-inch allowance to the wrong side of the fabric, and staple the fabric to the back of the Back piece. If you use this method, cover the Support Strip with matching fabric. Attach the upholstered plywood pieces to the PVC frame, using long wood screws inserted first through the frame and into the plywood.

3. Put the Seat in place (**Figure D**) and attach it to the front and rear crosspieces of the bar stool frame, using two molly bolts for each joint.

4. Use the piece of scrap lumber (¾ x ¾ x 14½ inches) as the Support Strip. The Back and Support Strip are placed as shown in **Figure D**. Glue the Support Strip to the Seat and secure it using two of the wood screws.

5. Use the remaining two wood screws to attach the Back to the Support Strip. In addition, insert two molly bolts through the Back, into the upper crosspiece of the frame.

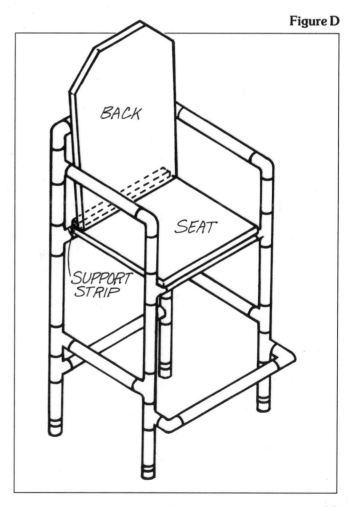

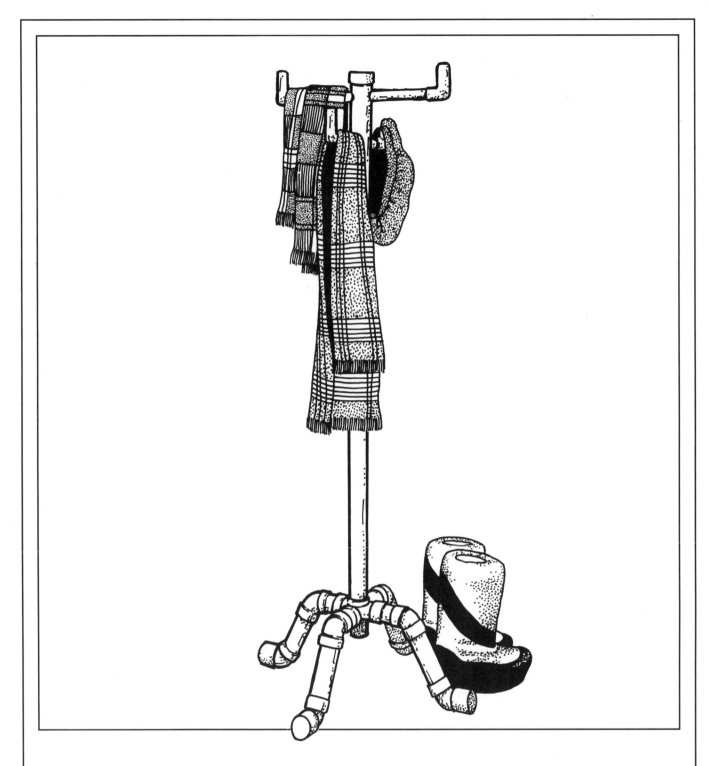

Coat Rack

Here's a freestanding rack for all your coats, hats, and other hangups. It's 70 inches tall, with a sure-footed 23-inch-square base and a generous set of hangers.

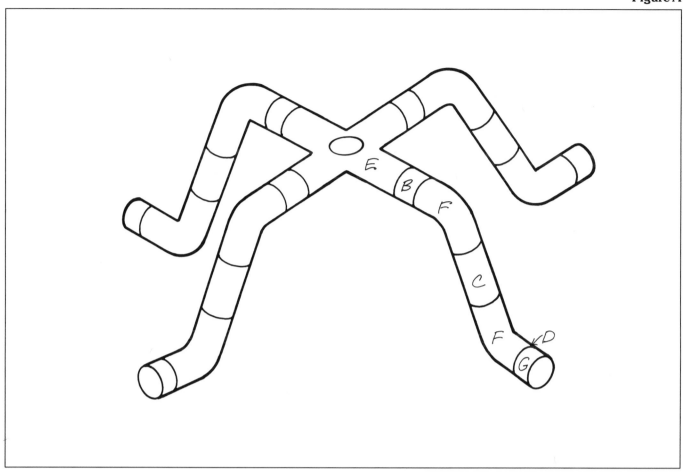

Materials

9 feet of 1½-inch straight PVC pipe.

3 feet of ¾-inch straight CPVC pipe.

1½-inch PVC fittings: eight 60-degree angle joints, one double-T joint, and seven end caps.

¾-inch CPVC fittings: four 90-degree angle joints and four end caps.

PVC solvent cement; or fifty No. 6 gauge self-tapping sheet metal screws, each 1 inch long, and twenty-five, each ¾ inch long.

Cutting the pipe

1. The lengths of 1½-inch straight pipe listed below were calculated on the basis of ¾-inch fitting allowances. Check the depth of the fittings you purchased and, if necessary, recalculate the lengths of pipe to compensate for the difference on each end. Cut and label the pieces of straight pipe. Label the 1½-inch fittings as listed at right, above.

Part	Length	Quantity
A	5¼ feet	1
B	2¾ inches	4
C	6¼ inches	4
D	1⅜ inches	4

Fittings:

E	Double-T joint
F	60-degree joint
G	End cap

2. The lengths of ¾-inch straight pipe listed below were calculated on the basis of ¾-inch fitting allowances. Check the depth of the fittings you purchased and, if necessary, recalculate the lengths of pipe to compensate for the difference on each end. Cut and label the pieces of straight pipe. Label the ¾-inch fittings as listed below.

Part	Length	Quantity
H	11 inches	1
J	15 inches	1
K	1⅜ inches	4

Fittings:

L	90-degree angle joint
M	End cap

Assembly

The frame consists of four sections: a base section (**Figure A**), a pole section (**Figure B**), and two hanger sections (**Figure C**). The assembled frame is shown in **Figure F**.

147

Figure C

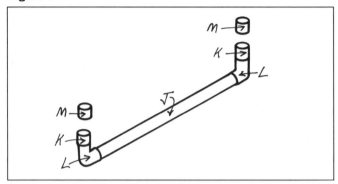

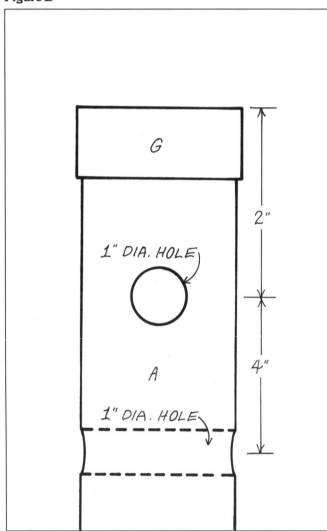

Figure D

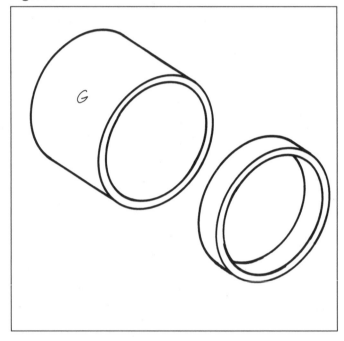

2. Assemble three more identical leg portions, as in step 1.

3. Find the center of the **E** fitting and drill a 1⅞-inch diameter hole all the way through both sides.

4. To assemble the base, slip the **B** piece of each leg portion into one open end of the **E** fitting (**Figure A**).

Assembling the pole and hangers

1. The pole section is shown in **Figure B**. Begin by inserting one end of the **A** piece into a **G** fitting. Drill a 1-inch-diameter hole all the way through the **A** piece, 2 inches from the top. Drill another 1-inch-diameter hole all the way through the **A** piece, 4 inches below the first hole and perpendicular to it (**Figure B**).

2. One hanger section is shown in **Figure C**. Insert each end of the **J** piece into an **L** fitting. Make sure both **L** fittings are turned in the same direction. Use a **K** piece to connect an **M** fitting to the end of each **L** fitting.

3. To create the second hanger section, repeat the procedures in step 2 using the **H** piece in place of the **J** piece.

Building the base section

1. The base section is shown in **Figure** A. It consists of four identical leg portions connected to a central **E** fitting. Begin by assembling one leg portion as shown. Attach an **F** fitting to each end of a **C** piece, turning the fittings in opposite directions. Attach a **G** fitting to one of the **F** fittings, using a short **D** piece. Insert a **B** piece into the **F** fitting at the opposite end of the leg.

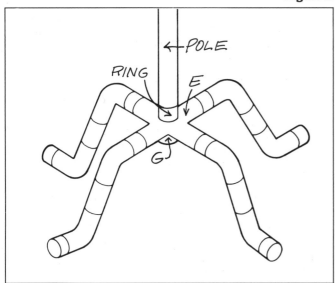

Final assembly

The completed rack, with base, pole, and hanger sections assembled, is shown in **Figure F**.

1. First, you will need to modify one of the **G** fittings. To do this, simply slice a ½-inch-wide ring off the open end as shown in **Figure D**. Keep the ring. You will not need the rest of the cap.

2. The ring will serve as a washer to help stabilize the pole section where it will meet the base. Slide the ring onto the lower end of the pole section.

3. A detail diagram of the base-to-pole assembly is shown in **Figure E**. First, slide the ring a short way up toward the top of the pole section. Insert the lower end of the pole section all the way through the hole in the central **E** fitting of the base section. Install the remaining **G** fitting on the lower end of the **A** piece and then slide the ring down until it rests on top of the base section, as shown. Glue the pole in place.

4. Install the hanger sections at the top of the pole, as shown in **Figure F**. To install the first hanger section, temporarily remove the fitting assembly from one end of the straight center piece. Insert the free end of the center piece through the upper holes in the pole and reinstall the fitting assembly on the end. Adjust the hanger section so it extends equally on each side of the pole.

5. Repeat the procedures in step 4 to install the remaining hanger section through the lower holes in the pole section (**Figure F**).

149

Cat House

Domicile your favorite feline in style! This charming abode consists of a very simple pipe frame and a padded muslin cover that is decorated with appliqued designs. It is a 16-inch cube. The fabric roof adds 12 inches to the height.

Materials

For the frame:

10 feet of ¾-inch straight CPVC pipe.

¾-inch CPVC fittings: four T-joints, and eight 90-degree angle joints.

CPVC solvent cement or self-tapping screws (optional).

For the cover:

3 yards of unbleached muslin.

1½ yards of bright-colored fabric for the roof. We used a rust-colored polished cotton.

Scraps of calico and solid-color fabrics for the flower and mailbox appliques.

1 yard of ¼-inch-wide ribbon and 1 yard of ¾-inch-wide double-fold bias tape in colors that coordinate with the roof and applique fabrics.

1 yard of green single-fold seam-binding tape or ¾-inch-wide ribbon.

One package of quilt batting.

Small amount of polyester fiberfill.

7 x 13-inch piece of cardboard.

14 yards of yellow, brown, or white yarn for the bird's nest.

Heavy-duty and regular sewing thread, white glue, scissors, pins, water soluble marking pen, sewing machine (optional), and pattern paper.

Building the frame

The frame consists of two identical rectangular sections (**Figure B**) that are connected by two straight pieces of pipe. The entire assembled frame is shown in **Figure A**.

1. The required lengths of straight pipe listed below were calculated on the basis of ½-inch-long fitting allowances. Check the depth of the fittings and, if necessary, recalculate each length of pipe to compensate for the difference on each end. The fittings are listed here with code letters for purposes of identification in the assembly.

Part	Length	Quantity
A	1 foot	6
B	6 inches	8
Fittings:		
C	90-degree joint	
D	T-joint	

2. An assembly diagram of one rectangular section is provided in **Figure B**. Assemble the section, beginning with the **B**, **C**, and **D** pieces that form each vertical side. Be sure that the open ends of the fittings face the direction shown. When you have assembled the two vertical sides (which should be mirror images of each other), join them with the two **A** pieces to finish the section.

3. Make another rectangular section just like the first one.

4. Use the two remaining **A** pieces to join the two sections as shown in **Figure A**.

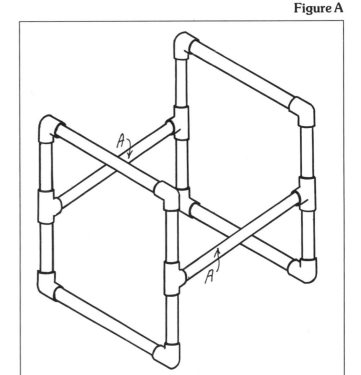

Figure A

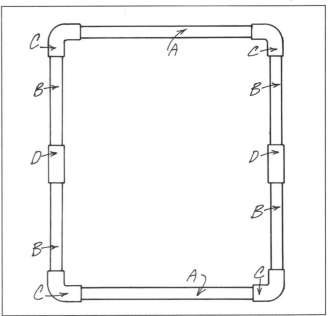

Figure B

151

Figure F

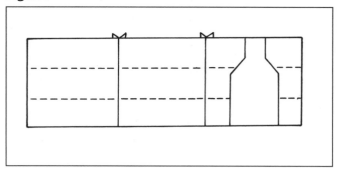

Figure C

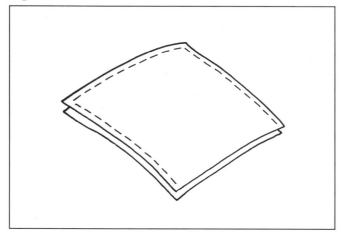

Figure D

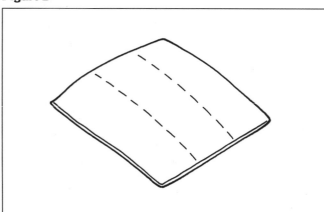

Figure E

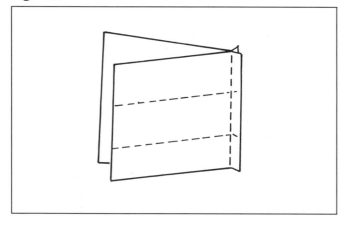

Making the cover panels

Note: All seam allowances are ¼ inch unless otherwise specified. We suggest that you wash and dry the muslin before cutting the pieces, to allow for shrinkage.

1. The frame is covered by a fabric "box" that consists of six panels: front, back, top, bottom, and two sides. Each panel is a double layer of muslin with quilt batting sandwiched between. Cut four 15½-inch squares of muslin for the front and back panels. Cut eight muslin rectangles, each 15½ x 16½ inches, for the remaining panels.

2. To make the front panel, pin two 15½-inch muslin squares right sides together and stitch the seams along three edges, leaving the fourth edge open and unstitched (**Figure C**). Clip the corners, turn the panel right side out, and press the seam allowances to the inside along the open raw edge.

3. Use the assembled panel as a pattern to cut a square of quilt batting. Insert the batting inside the panel and whipstitch the opening edges together.

4. To make the back panel, repeat steps 2 and 3 using the two remaining 15½-inch muslin squares. Then use the eight muslin rectangles, two at a time, to make the top, bottom, and side panels in the same manner. Use several layers of batting inside the bottom panel.

5. On the back and side panels only, run two evenly-spaced lines of topstitching through all thicknesses from side to side as shown in **Figure D**. (On the side panels, "from side to side" is the longer distance.)

6. A chimney is appliqued to one side panel, and it's easier to do this now than after the cover is assembled. A scale drawing of the Chimney is provided in **Figure G**. Enlarge the drawing to full size and cut one Chimney from the bright-colored roof fabric. Press the seam allowances to the wrong side of the fabric on all edges, clipping corners and curves where necessary. Pin the Chimney to the right side of one side panel, in the center, and applique it in place. If you are doing the applique by hand, use a blind stitch or a closely-spaced blanket stitch. You may prefer to use a wide, closely-spaced machine zigzag stitch.

7. Pin one side panel to the back panel along one edge, placing right sides together and matching quilting lines. Stitch the seam (**Figure E**) and press it open. Attach the remaining side panel to the opposite edge of the back panel in the same manner. The right side of the finished assembly is shown in **Figure F**.

1 square = 1 inch

Figure G

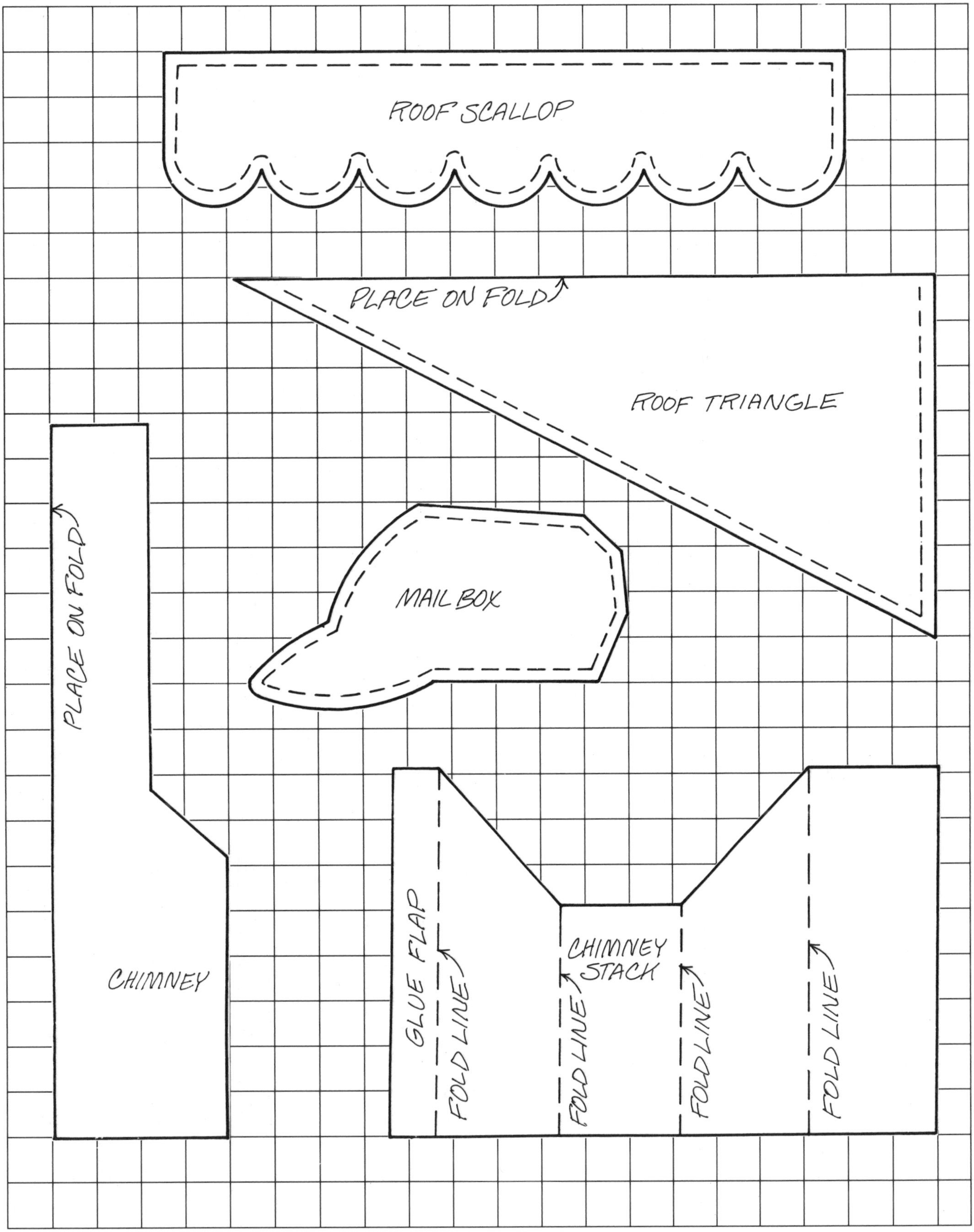
ROOF SCALLOP
PLACE ON FOLD
ROOF TRIANGLE
PLACE ON FOLD
MAIL BOX
CHIMNEY
GLUE FLAP
FOLD LINE
CHIMNEY STACK
FOLD LINE
FOLD LINE
FOLD LINE

Figure J

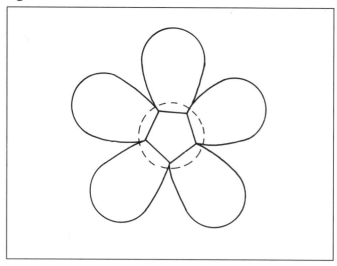

Figure H

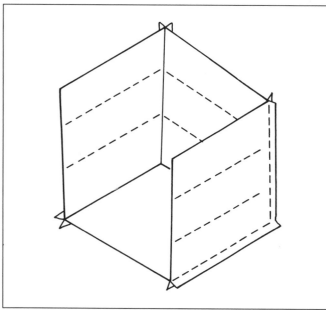

Figure I

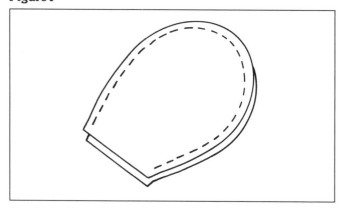

Finishing the front panel

1. The front panel contains a circular "door" and is decorated with two flowers and a mailbox. To make the front door, find a round plate or pan lid that is a good size for an opening for your cat. (A 6-inch-diameter circle should be large enough for all but the heftiest house cats.) Trace the outline of the plate in the center of the front panel and then stitch along the traced line using a short stitch.

2. Cut out the center of the circle, ¼ inch inside the stitching line. Encase the raw edge of the circular opening in double-fold bias tape, and stitch the tape in place.

3. We made two flowers for the front. Scale drawings for the flower parts (Petals and Center) are provided in **Figure K**. Enlarge the drawings to full size. For each flower, cut ten Petal pieces and two Center pieces from calico or solid-color fabric scraps.

4. Each flower has five petals. To make one petal, pin two Petal pieces right sides together and stitch the seam along the curved edge, leaving the short straight edge open (**Figure I**). Clip the curves, turn the stitched petal right side out, and whipstitch the straight raw edges together. Repeat these procedures to make the remaining petals.

5. For each flower, place one Center piece wrong side up on a flat surface. Pin the straight edge of one assembled petal to the Center piece, overlapping the edges by about ½ inch. Pin the remaining four petals around the Center piece in the same manner, overlapping the petals if necessary. Stitch the seam ¼ inch from the edge of the Center piece (**Figure J**).

6. Place a small amount of fiberfill in the middle of the Center piece, on top of the edges of the petals. Place the remaining Center piece right side up over the fiberfill, and whipstitch it in place, folding the raw edge under as you sew. Put the completed flower blossoms aside for the time being.

7. The mailbox applique consists of three pieces: the Mailbox, a Stand, and an Insert. A scale drawing for the Mailbox piece is provided in **Figure G**; drawings for the Stand and Insert in **Figure K**. Enlarge the drawings and cut one of each piece from fabric scraps. The Insert should be light-colored.

8. Fold the side panels forward so that the assembly is in a square "C" shape, with the right sides of the panels facing inward. Pin the bottom panel to the lower edge of this assembly, placing right sides together (**Figure H**), and stitch the seam along each edge.

9. Pin and stitch the top panel to the outside edges of the back and side panels in the same manner. You should now have a fabric box with an open front.

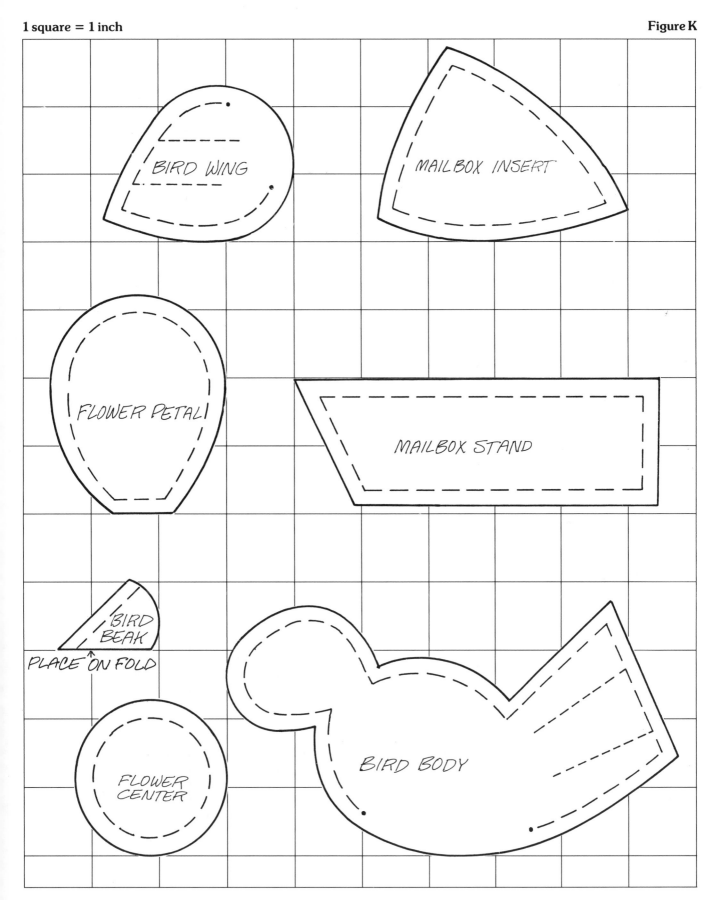

BIRD WING

MAILBOX INSERT

FLOWER PETAL

MAILBOX STAND

BIRD BEAK

PLACE ON FOLD

FLOWER CENTER

BIRD BODY

Figure L

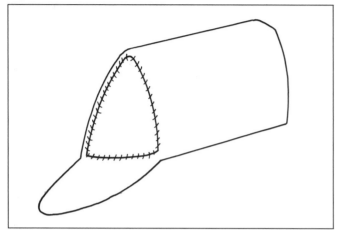

Figure M

Figure N

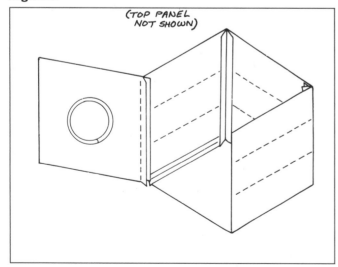
(TOP PANEL NOT SHOWN)

Figure O

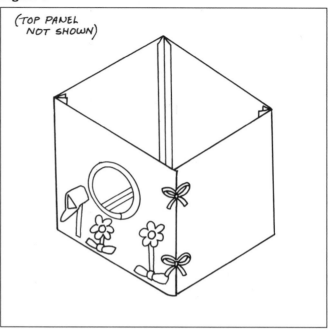
(TOP PANEL NOT SHOWN)

8. To prepare the Mailbox and Insert pieces, press the seam allowances to the wrong side of the fabric on all edges of each piece, clipping curves and corners. Applique the Insert to the Mailbox as shown in **Figure L**. This can be done by hand, using a blanket stitch or whipstitch, or by machine, using a zigzag stitch.

9. Pin the assembled mailbox and flower blossoms to the front panel as shown in **Figure M**. Pin the mailbox Stand in place, and applique the entire mailbox assembly to the panel. Add a little fiberfill underneath the mailbox if you like.

10. The stems and leaves of the flowers are made using green satin ribbon or single-fold seam tape. For the shorter flower, cut a 4-inch length of ribbon for the stem. Pin the stem in place below the flower blossom. Cut an 8-inch length of ribbon for the leaves, and fold both ends in to the center, folding wrong sides together. Overlap the ends slightly and tack them in place. Tack this double leaf to the bottom of the stem. Repeat these procedures to create a stem and leaves for the taller flower, using a 6-inch length of ribbon for the stem and a 10-inch length for the leaves.

11. Applique the flower stems to the panel. To secure the blossoms, stitch around the center portion only, leaving the petals free.

Attaching the front panel

1. The front panel is stitched to one of the side panels only. Ribbon ties secure the opposite edge to the other side panel, so the cover can be removed from the frame easily. Pin and stitch one edge of the front panel to the partially assembled cover, placing right sides together, as shown in **Figure N**.

2. Cut four 6-inch lengths of ¼-inch-wide ribbon for the ties. Stitch two ties to the free side edge of the front panel. Stitch the remaining two ties to the side panel (**Figure O**).

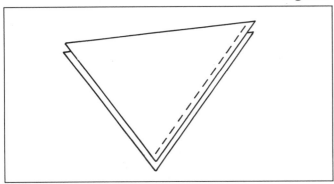

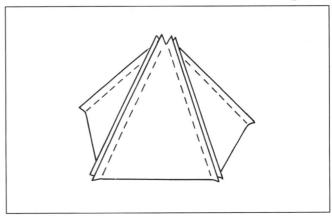

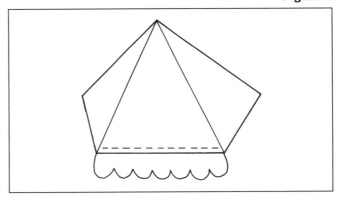

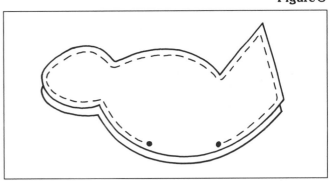

Making the roof

1. Scale drawings of the Roof Triangle and Scallop Trim are provided in **Figure G**. Enlarge the drawings to make full-size patterns. Cut eight Roof Triangles and eight Scallops from the bright-colored fabric.

2. Four of the Triangle pieces are sewn together to form the pitched roof. Pin two of the Triangles together along one long edge, placing right sides together, and stitch the seam (**Figure P**). Press the seam open. Stitch another Triangle to the other long edge of the first Triangle in the same manner. Add the fourth Triangle by stitching it to both free long edges of this assembly in the same manner, so you have a pyramid shape (**Figure Q**).

3. To make a roof lining, repeat the procedures described in step 2, using the remaining four Triangle pieces.

4. Use the Roof Triangle pattern to cut four pieces of quilt batting for the roof.

5. Pin the assembled roof and lining wrong sides together with the batting pieces sandwiched between the two layers. "Stitch in the ditch" (along the existing seams) by hand, through all thicknesses, to secure the batting. Press the seam allowances to the inside along the lower raw edges. Whipstitch the pressed edges of the lining and roof together along each side.

6. The scallop trim serves as a canopy on each side of the lower roof edge. Pin two Scallop pieces right sides together. Stitch the seam along the scalloped edge, leaving the straight edge open and unstitched. Clip the curves and corners, turn the stitched scallop right side out, and press. Finish the raw edges by either pinking, zigzagging, or pressing the seam allowances to the inside. Pin the straight edge of this assembly to the lining side of the roof along one edge. Hand or machine stitch the trim in place (**Figure R**). Repeat these procedures to form and attach three additional roof trim sections, using the remaining six Scallop pieces.

7. A scale drawing of the Chimney Stack is provided in **Figure G**. Enlarge the drawing and cut one Chimney Stack from cardboard. Fold the cardboard along the dotted lines indicated on the drawing, making all folds in the same direction. Spread glue on the outside of the narrow glue flap and attach it to the inside of the opposite edge.

8. Cover the cardboard base with bright-colored fabric, folding the raw edges of the fabric to the inside of the base and glueing the fabric in place. Glue or whipstitch the assembled chimney stack to the roof, aligning it over the chimney that is appliqued on one side panel of the cover. Place the assembled roof on top of the house.

Making the bird and nest

1. Scale drawings of the Bird Body, Wing, and Beak are provided in **Figure K**. Enlarge the drawings to full size. Cut two Bird pieces and four Wings (we used light blue fabric), and cut one Beak from yellow fabric. Transfer the small dots and the dotted sculpture lines to the fabric using a water soluble marking pen.

2. Pin the two Body pieces right sides together. Stitch the seam around the outer edge, leaving it open between the small dots (**Figure S**). Clip the curves and corners, turn the

Figure W

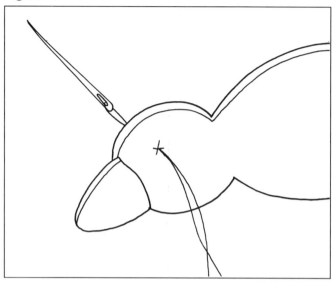

Figure T

Figure U

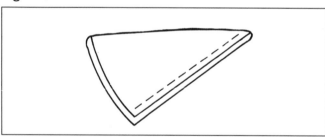

Figure V

bird right side out, and press. Press the seam allowances to the inside along the opening edges. Stuff the bird with fiberfill and whipstitch the opening edges together. To create the "tail feathers," topstitch along the sculpture lines on the tail through all thicknesses.

3. Pin two Wing pieces right sides together. Stitch the seam around the outer edge, leaving it open between the small dots. Clip the curves, turn the stitched wing right side out, and press. Press the seam allowances to the inside along the opening edges. Stuff the wing with fiberfill but do not stitch the opening edges together. To create the "feathers," topstitch along the sculpture lines through all thicknesses. Make a second wing in the same manner.

4. To attach one wing to the bird, shape the wing opening into an oval and pin the opening edge to one side of the bird (**Figure T**). Whipstitch around the edge to secure the wing so that it extends out from the body in a "takeoff" position. Attach the second wing to the opposite side of the body in the same manner.

5. Fold the Beak piece in half, placing right sides together, and stitch the seam along the straight edge. Leave the slightly curved edge open and unstitched, so that you have a cone shape (**Figure U**). Turn the stitched beak right side out and press the seam allowance to the inside along the raw edge. Glue or whipstitch the beak to the front of the bird's head (**Figure V**).

6. To form the bird's eyes, use a long needle and a length of heavy-duty black thread. Take a few stitches back and forth through the head at eye level, just above and behind the beak (**Figure W**). Pull the thread gently until slight indentations appear on each side of the head, lock the stitch, and cut the thread.

7. To make the bird's nest, cut fifty strands of yarn, each 10 inches long. Gather the strands in the center and tie a short piece of yarn securely around them.

8. Place the nest in the top of the chimney stack, and put the bird in her nest. You can glue or stitch the nest and bird in place, or leave them unsecured.

End Table

It's a piece of cake, but totally inedible. This end table is truly easy, fast, and inexpensive to make, and you have a choice of materials for the tabletop. Overall dimensions are 14½ x 20 x 14 inches.

Figure A

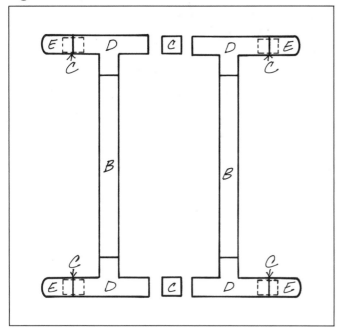

Figure B

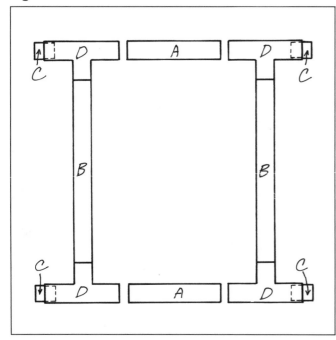

Figure C

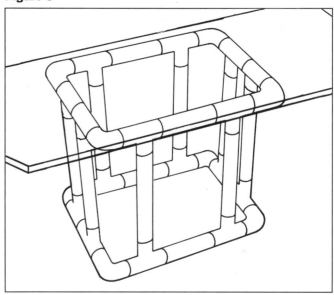

strong double-sided tape or attach nylon fastening strips to the tabletop and frame using epoxy glue. This allows you to remove the top easily for cleaning. If you choose a wooden top, use 1-inch-long wood screws (you'll need four), or use one of the fastening materials described for the acrylic top.

Assembly

The table consists of four sections: two identical side sections (**Figure A**), and identical front and back sections (**Figure B**).

1. Cut and label the lengths of pipe listed below. The fitting allowance used to calculate the lengths was ¾ inch. Check the depth of each fitting and recalculate the lengths, if necessary, to compensate for the difference on each end. Label the fittings as listed.

Part	Length	Quantity
A	6¼ inches	4
B	12½ inches	8
C	1½ inches	20
Fittings:		
D	T-joint	
E	90-degree joint	

2. Begin by assembling one side section as shown in **Figure A**. Assemble the two separate portions and then join them, using two short **C** pieces as shown.

3. Assemble an identical side section.

4. Assemble the front section as shown in **Figure B**. Begin with the two separate side portions and then join them, using the **A** pieces.

5. Assemble an identical back section.

6. Now simply join the front and back sections to the two side sections. The assembled table is shown in **Figure C**.

7. Attach the tabletop, using the method you have chosen.

Materials

14 feet of straight 1-inch PVC pipe.

1-inch PVC fittings: sixteen T-joints and eight 90-degree angle joints.

PVC solvent cement or 64 self-tapping sheet metal screws, each ½ inch long.

Tabletop: 14½ x 20-inch (or larger) piece of ½-inch plywood, waferwood, or acrylic sheet.

Fasteners: You have several options for attaching the table- top to the pipe frame. If you choose an acrylic top, use